CRASH COURSE

on
Getting Things Done Now

17
PROVEN
PRINCIPLES
FOR
OVERCOMING
PROCRASTINATION

A Division of Thomas Nelson Publishers
Since 1798

www.thomasnelson.com

Published by J. Countryman® a division of Thomas Nelson, Inc., Nashville, Tennessee 37214

Written by Lisa Tresch

www.jcountryman.com
www.thomasnelson.com

Designed by Randall Miller Design, Tulsa, Oklahoma

ISBN 1-4041-8656-5

Printed in China

CRASH COURSE

on
Getting Things Done Now

17
PROVEN
PRINCIPLES
FOR
OVERCOMING
PROCRASTINATION

Table of Contents

Introduction

To the Reader:

What a wonderful thing it would be to vanquish procrastination! Procrastination is the gremlin in the night that booby-traps the road to our success and snacks on our self-esteem. Not only that, empty promises in lieu of timely action gets people really angry at you when important deadlines are unmet.

But I really don't have to mention these things to you, now, do I? That's why you picked up this book. You have experienced the problems and consequences caused by your chronic (and highly inventive) delay tactics and you have vowed to find a path out of the quagmire.

Well, congratulations: You've found it! This book is an absolutely wonderful guide to overcoming procrastination. First, and very importantly, you will find that you are not alone in this affliction. Some really successful people have struggled with procrastination. Second, you will find out the root causes of the problem. Understanding and knowledge is critical in the process to recovery. Third, you get a step-by-step plan to get you on your very own path to vanquishing your proclivity to drag your feet.

Sounds good, doesn't it? It gets even better, though. The prize for your effort will be dramatic. You will:

- Gain the trust of your family, friends, and business associates.

- Avoid the always-present underlying anxiety of looming consequences.

- Banish the guilt over flimsy and fabricated excuses, not to mention out-and-out lies.

- Get to be at the dock when your ship comes in.

- Stop the erosion of personal relationships.

- Build your self-confidence and bask in its glow.

- Put yourself on the super highway to success in life.

Deep in your heart, you have always wanted to rid yourself of this problem. It has plagued you and limited your life longer than you remember. So now is the time. A solution is before you. All you need to do is begin!

Good Luck!

Larry J. Koenig, Ph.D.
Series Consultant and General Editor

P.S. This is a wonderfully well-written book filled with interesting and useful information! My kudos to the author, Lisa Tresch.

CHAPTER 1

In Favor of Tomorrow

Nothing is so fatiguing as the eternal hanging on of an uncompleted task.

—WILLIAM JAMES

POWER STATEMENT:

Procrastination is a problem that brings about stress and guilt and makes life more complicated than it should be.

The desk is clean. The papers are filed. You've sharpened pencils, put new batteries in the clock, checked your e-mail several times, and made fresh coffee. You're ready to start the project that's been in front of you for three days. You turn to glance out the window before you get started and notice the cobwebs. Someone should clean those windowsills—and the baseboards could use a good dusting, too. The project waits forlornly on the clean desk beside the sharpened pencils and the coffee mug and the ticking clock.

If this scene sounds familiar, you're not alone. Twenty-five percent of the population identify themselves as chronic procrastinators, and some research suggests up to 70 percent of people have a serious problem with procrastination.[1] The college student who just can't seem to get started on that mid-term paper has something in common with the grandmother who waits until two days before Christmas to start her holiday shopping. At some point, all of us have succumbed to the lure of putting off that looming chore, project, or assignment until another hour or another day.

The illustration of the procrastinator who just can't seem to get started is a familiar one. Sitting down to do the job seems to bring about all kinds of reminders of far more urgent, usually menial things that simply *must* be done before the real job can begin. Writers know this all too well. With a blank page before them, suddenly they discover an urgent need to make a phone call, color-coordinate paper clips, sharpen scissors.

The word *procrastination* comes from the Latin "pro," which means "forth, or forward," and "crastinus," meaning "tomorrow." The Oxford dictionary defines it as "deferring or delaying action, intentionally or habitually." The writer Napoleon Hill puts it this way: "Procrastination is the bad habit of putting of until the day after tomorrow what should have been done the day before yesterday."

For the procrastinator, the task before them begins with good intentions. They make a plan and have high hopes about the success of fulfilling it, but when the time comes to actually get started, they can't seem to clear the hurdle. Tomorrow always seems to be a better day to begin.

If you can relate to any of

DID YOU KNOW?

Hesiod is one of the first recorded poets of Greek literature. In one of his poems, he provides one of the first citations of the problem of procrastination:
Do not put your work off till tomorrow and the day after; for a sluggish worker does not fill his barn, nor one who puts off his work: industry makes work go well, but a man who puts off work is always hand-grips with ruin (Works and Days, l. 413).

the following statements, you probably fall into the ranks of a procrastinator:

- You always return videos with cash in hand to cover the late fee.

- Your house or apartment is cluttered with half-finished projects.

- When it's time to start a big job, you find all kinds of little jobs that must be done before you can begin.

- You wrap Christmas presents on Christmas morning.

- You're reluctant to take risks or try something new.

- You buy boxes of stationery and thank-you and birthday cards, but never get around to sending them.

- Your enthusiasm for a task wanes when it comes to actually starting it.

- Deadlines make you feel paralyzed.

- The deadlines usually don't get met.

A classic example of a procrastinator is Chris, who volunteered to organize her family's summer reunion picnic one year. She took on the project with excitement and even sat down with pen and paper to make some plans, but then decided it was actually too early to start planning. She'd get started in a couple of weeks, she told herself.

But Chris found quite a few other things to do. She cleaned closets and surfed the Internet and rearranged the furniture in her living room. The weeks turned into a couple of months and before she realized it, Chris had backed herself into an impossible corner. The deadline was closing in on her like a nasty storm, and so she spent the weeks before the reunion biting her nails, losing sleep, and turning in circles. Procrastinating left her feeling stressed and resentful that she had taken the project on in the first place. The picnic was thrown together in time, but Chris and everyone else in the family felt the effects of procrastination. At the end of it all, she was left with an overwhelming sense of guilt.

Psychologists agree that the reasons people procrastinate are many and varied. According to Dr. Kevin Austin, psychologist at California Institute of Technology, the causes of procrastination are not always obvious.[2] Although it may look like laziness or a lack of willpower, procrastination is often something quite different. Chris, who took on the task of organizing the reunion picnic with great enthusiasm, may have experienced a fear of failure when it came to actually completing the project. Her tendency toward perfection may have immobilized her and caused her to worry that the planning process and the picnic itself might not be flawless.

Some people argue that they work better under pressure. David, a college student, delayed starting a mid-term paper because he convinced himself that starting the paper too early would diminish its quality. "My creative process works best when I'm closer to the finish line," was his excuse. His professor knew better, and was not surprised to see that David's paper was mediocre. David, however, was certain that his procrastination tactic pumped his creative juices. What he didn't realize is that he was only working feverishly because he didn't have a choice.

Procrastinators usually know who they are. They live with the same consequences that Chris and David live with: stress and anxiety, impossible deadlines, feelings of bitterness and resentment, guilt, and low-quality results. They're experts at making excuses and fall into the pattern of telling themselves little white lies like, "I'm too tired to get started on that right now," or "I'll save that for later when I have more time."

For procrastinators, life doesn't seem to work as well as

FAST FACTS:

Research has shown that 70 percent of New Year's resolutions are abandoned by February 1.

it should, yet they find themselves in a cycle they can't seem to break. Since procrastination has such a negative impact on job performance, relationships, self-esteem, and health, it seems implausible that procrastination would remain such a pervasive problem—we should be smart enough to figure out that we should never engage in activity with such damaging results. Yet procrastination continues to sneak up on us, tempting us with the notion that tomorrow is a better day to begin.

If you're reading this book (and with good intentions of finishing it!), you have probably already determined that procrastination is affecting your life in some way. This crash course will help you identify some of the causes of procrastination and understand the principles for overcoming it.

Deciding to stop procrastinating is not simply a matter of making a promise to do things differently. As the saying goes, habit is overcome by habit. It takes repeated efforts to replace the bad habits with good habits. By incorporating the principles in this book consistently and diligently, you can drive out the negative habits that cause procrastination and replace them with habits that help you get the job done *now*. There are probably all kinds of things you could look around and find to do besides read this book, but don't save it for tomorrow. Today is a much better day to begin.

Leonardo da Vinci was one of history's most famous procrastinators. He never finished a project on time, and was notorious for jumping from one unfinished endeavor to another. His painting *Mona Lisa* took twenty years to complete and *The Last Supper* was finished only after his patron threatened to cut off funds. He planned to write three books on mathematical subjects, but they were never published. His notebooks were filled with ingenious inventions and machines; most were never built or implemented. On his death bed he apologized to "God and Man for leaving so much undone."

PERSONAL REFLECTION:

Write down three projects or tasks that you had good intentions of starting, but have yet to begin.

What excuses have you used for not starting or completing these projects or tasks?

What negative affects have you experienced from procrastinating?

✓ YOUR TO DO LIST:

Choose one of the three project or tasks that you listed above, write it on an index card, and determine that you will put into practice the principles outlined in this book to help you complete it. Use the index card as a bookmark or post it conspicuously in your work area.

FOR FURTHER STUDY:

What's Your Sabotage?
      by Alyce Cornyn-Selby

How to Get Control of Your Time and Your Life
      by Alan Lakein

What's *Your* Excuse?

My evil genius Procrastination has whispered me to tarry 'til a more convenient season.

—MARY TODD LINCOLN

POWER STATEMENT:

Excuses are little white lies we tell ourselves to perpetuate the procrastination cycle.

Procrastinators are hopeful people. At the beginning of a project or chore, they really believe that they will get the job done. They talk about it and make plans and then talk about it a little more. They make a few more plans, do a little more talking, but eventually there is a time when they can do no more planning and talking. It's time to start. And that's when the excuses kick in.

Every procrastinator is a pro at making excuses. These are the pegs that the delaying process hangs on. If you can't come up with a good reason to put it off, then you're stuck with the frightening possibility that you might have to get started. Excuses are vital to the procrastinator. In fact, most procrastinators have more than one that they can pull out of the bag for a variety of occasions.

If you have determined that you want to end the procrastination cycle, then you should be forewarned that this chapter may bring out into the open and expose all those flimsy excuses you've been using. And that's the first step in eliminating the procrastination habit—to recognize the excuses for what they are.

SO HERE, IN DESCENDING ORDER, ARE THE TOP TEN FAVORITE EXCUSES OF THE PROCRASTINATOR:

10. "I need time to think this through before I get started."

Procrastinators like to ponder the job that is before them. Thinking about it is a whole lot easier than starting it. Sometimes the pondering process can take days, or weeks, or months. For some people, it can take years.

June had always dreamed of going back to school to get a master's degree. She thought about how it would help her get a better job. She thought about how it might increase her earning potential. She thought about how fulfilling it would be to reach that goal. June did quite a bit of thinking. She told herself that she needed to look at the opportunity from many different angles before she began the application process. For fifteen years, June thought about it. Her procrastination was a thought-filled process, but it didn't get her anywhere.

9. "I never have enough time to just have fun. I'll celebrate tonight and start later."

This excuse works well for a short-term delay. The procrastinator usually spends so much time and effort putting things off, it's probably true that he doesn't have enough time for fun. It also perpetuates the "poor me" mentality, which is important to the procrastinator because it helps him believe his own excuses.

The celebration, however, is a short one. Hanging over

the procrastinator's head is the knowledge that there is a job to be started. Once he's had a few days of fun, the excuse begins to wear thin. After all, you can't keep telling yourself that you never have enough time for fun if you've been playing for several weeks. So although this excuse is an effective one, it can't be used very long. The procrastinator has to move on to something more believable.

8. "I need to get organized before I start."

At the prospect of starting the task or project, some procrastinators abruptly transform into organizational fanatics. The desk must be rearranged, drawers cleaned out, and files alphabetized—again. This organizational busywork helps delay the starting process while at the same time giving the procrastinator the satisfying sensation that she is accomplishing something. This excuse has the added benefit of making the procrastinator look productive. At first glance, people might think she's really getting down to the job instead of just doing organizational piddling.

7. "This is too hard."

Ted's New Year's resolution was to begin a savings plan for retirement. He even wrote down his resolution with a four-step plan: research, open a retirement account, scale back spending, and put money in the account. He managed to do some research, which gave him the momentum to open the account. Confident that he was on a roll, he promised himself that he would continue his resolution and scale back spending. But then something awful happened: Ted decided that keeping within his budget was a really hard thing to do, and all his momentum came to a grinding halt.

When his retirement account statement arrived in the mail each month, he looked at it and decided it might be easier to save for retirement after his next raise. The excuse worked. At the beginning of every year, Ted *thought* about saving for retirement, but then he reminded himself that it was just too hard.

6. "I'm not in the mood."

Waiting until the mood strikes is always an effective way to procrastinate, because chances are the mood won't strike at the right time. The fortunate procrastinator gets a whim to begin the project when she is commuting, or in the shower, or hang gliding. If the mood doesn't strike while she is sitting at her desk or at a convenient place to begin the project, then she'll just have to keep waiting. Some procrastinators aren't really sure what the mood feels like, but they're confident they'll recognize it when it hits them.

5. "I'll go ahead and eat this. I'm starting my diet tomorrow."

Tomorrow is the procrastinator's favorite day. It's a better day to start anything, especially a diet. They have high hopes for tomorrow and can envision themselves accomplishing great things, fulfilling promises, reaching goals—as long it falls within the realm of tomorrow.

A permanent sign in front of a restaurant says, "Free breakfast tomorrow." That's the truth of this excuse: Tomorrow is a day that never arrives. If today isn't a good day to start, then chances are tomorrow won't be any better, and the excuse continues.

4. "I have other things to do first."

The procrastinator gets a multitude of things accomplished before he settles down to actually start what he really *should* be doing. If the main task is to clean closets, he'll dust the bookshelves. If the main task is to dust the bookshelves, he'll clean the closets.

Most procrastinators don't audibly voice this excuse ahead of time. It seems to come out of nowhere as soon as it is time to begin the project. Take Ben, for example, who was supposed to spend Saturday morning filling out his tax forms. He poured some coffee and sat down at the computer. In a matter of minutes he was back up again because before he could get started, he needed to empty the dishwasher. After all, lunch was only four hours away and he would need some clean dishes. After unloading the dishwasher, he sat back down and quickly remembered that he needed to sweep the leaves out of the garage. It would get too warm later in the day. Better to knock it out early. Ben found eight jobs that needed to get done before he sat down to do the tax forms, and by that time he had another excuse ready and waiting: He was tired.

3. "I'm too tired to start this now."

Everyone seems tired these days, especially the procrastinator. He looks at the job to be done, and all of his good intentions vanish in the fog of fatigue. He tells himself that he'll begin the job when he is fresh and rested. Most of the time, however, he doesn't do much to combat his tiredness. According to the National Sleep Foundation, almost 74 percent of Americans don't get enough sleep each night. We sleep an average of 6.9 hours a night, almost an hour less than a few decades ago.

Although this excuse may have some truth to it, the procrastinator can almost always find the energy to do many other things to delay the starting process, but when it comes to starting the task, weariness sets in.

2. "I have plenty of time."

Time is always the enemy of the procrastinator. She defies it, taunts it, ignores it, and really believes that she can control it—until she realizes that she has run out of it. If the report is due in a week, starting it seven days before the deadline is almost impossible. It's too easy to put it off with all that time stretched out endlessly in front of her.

Procrastinators rarely beat the deadline. A skewed perspective of time causes them to delay until there is little time left to finish.

1. "I work best under pressure."

This is the king of all procrastination excuses. It sounds so intentional, so thoughtful. The procrastinator seems to be concerned about the quality of the work, and therefore has made a conscious decision to begin at the last possible moment. In truth, this excuse causes the quality of the work to be poor, and sometimes assures that the job never gets done at all.

Bruce had a report due, but he decided to bring it down to the wire and work all day Thursday and into the evening because he "worked best

DID YOU KNOW?

A recent study found that procrastination peaks in the middle to late twenties, decreases for the next forty years and then increases again in the sixties.[1]

under pressure." Bruce didn't take into account all the things that could go wrong on Thursday, like a dead car battery and a call from the school telling him his son had a high fever. Now he was really working under pressure. He cranked out the report in the wee hours of Friday morning, but it was sloppy and filled with errors.

Most of the time, the procrastinator is making excuses to himself and not to other people. This self-talk becomes reality as the cycle of procrastination continues. Even when the excuses don't hold up, the procrastinator will use them over and over because they give him a reason to continue the behavior. And so, even though it's difficult, recognizing these excuses as little white lies is the first step in slaying the dragon of procrastination.

FAST FACTS:

In a study conducted by **Dr. Joseph Ferrari** of DePaul University, data presented about student excuses for late schoolwork found that 2.7 percent admitted to having falsely claimed that a grandmother had died. More common frauds include claims that the student's computer had failed or that a paper had been left behind in a dorm room. Dr. Ferrari found that students were significantly more likely to offer such lies to female rather than male instructors.

PERSONAL REFLECTION:

Review the excuses you wrote down from Chapter 1 for not starting or completing a project or task. Challenge each excuse by writing a reason why it is not valid.

✓ YOUR TO DO LIST:

As you seek to complete the project you chose in Chapter 1, listen for the excuses that will sneak into your thought process. Go back and review the challenges you wrote down for each excuse, and determine that you will not believe those "little white lies."

FOR FURTHER STUDY:

Excuses, Excuses: How to Spot Them, Deal With Them, and Stop Using Them
    —by Sven Wahlroos

Life Strategies: Do What Works, Do What Matters
    —by Phillip C. McGraw

CHAPTER 3

The Price of Putting It Off

Even if you're on the right track,
you'll get run over if you just sit there.

WILL ROGERS

POWER STATEMENT:

Procrastination can seem like a harmless habit, but it has negative and sometimes long-lasting consequences.

n anonymous procrastinator penned this creed:

1. *I believe that if anything is worth doing, it would have been done already.*

2. *I shall never move quickly, except to avoid more work or find excuses.*

3. *I will never rush into a job without a lifetime of consideration.*

4. *I shall meet all of my deadlines directly in proportion to the amount of bodily injury I could expect to receive from missing them.*

5. *I firmly believe that tomorrow holds the possibility for new technologies, astounding discoveries, and a reprieve from my obligations.*

6. *I truly believe that all deadlines are unreasonable regardless of the amount of time given.*

7. *I shall never forget that the probability of a miracle, though infinitely small, is not exactly zero.*

8. *If at first I don't succeed, there's always next year.*

9. *I shall always decide not to decide, unless of course I decide to change my mind.*

10. *I shall always begin, start, initiate, take the first* *step, and/or write the first word, when I get around to it.*

11. *I obey the law of inverse excuses which demands that the greater the task to be done, the more insignificant the work that must be done prior to beginning the greater task.*

12. *I know that the true work cycle is not plan/start/finish, but is wait/plan/plan.*

13. *I will never put off until tomorrow, what I can forget about forever.*

14. *I will become a member of the ancient Order of Two-Headed Turtles (the Procrastinator's Society)—if they ever get it organized.*

If you have been abiding by this creed for too long, now is the time to change your behavior. But that's easier said than done, because procrastination has a certain innocent charm about it. Promising yourself that you will start tomorrow seems harmless enough. What's the danger in a little delay?

Just ask Phil, who never filed that amended tax return. He missed out on receiving his refund which would have helped pay down that nasty credit card balance. Now his credit report is keeping him from getting a decent loan on that car he really needs to buy to replace the high-mileage car he's been driving for ten years. And on it goes. Phil has a literal price to pay for his procrastination.

Any negative behavior can have long-lasting effects that we can't see until it is too late, and procrastination is no exception. We may tell ourselves that there is no harm in putting it off, but there is always a price to pay, whether it is in actual dollars or in ways that are not so tangible. Here are a few of those price tags:

• Loss of Trust from Peers

Sometimes, everyone can see the ugliness of procrastination except the procrastinator. Like the emperor in his new clothes, he struts along thinking that he looks pretty good, yet everyone can see right through the empty promises and flimsy excuses. Trust tends to erode when people hear the same excuse over and over. And what about those manufactured reasons for not having the project in on time (how many times can you tell the boss you had to tend to your ailing aunt before he begins to catch on)? Word starts to get around. People whisper that perhaps the procrastinator is not the best person for the job. He can't be counted on to get things done on time, and if he does happen to make the deadline (a rarity), it's probably going to be shoddy work. It's hard to repair a bad reputation.

• Constant Anxiety

Even if the procrastinator can rush to meet the deadline and avoid serious penalties, he lives with a level of anxiety that is always churning beneath the surface. Putting things off is stressful. According to a study published in *Psychological Science* several years ago, college students who habitually procrastinated ended their semester with higher stress levels and in poorer health than students who did not procrastinate. Late in the semester, procrastinators reported an average of 8.2 symptoms per week, while the students who finished early only had 5.2 symptoms per week.[1]

Although the procrastinator may pull out his list of excuses for putting things off, the body is attuned to the negative effects of procrastination.

• Guilt

"I know I should have started this earlier." "I wish I hadn't wasted so much time." "I missed the deadline and now I've made a mess of the project."

The procrastinator is well aware of the guilt factor. She experiences it the most after she has backed herself into a corner or caused others to suffer because of her delays and failure to complete projects. She feels guilty for all the flimsy and fabricated excuses. She feels guilty because she has let other people down. She feels guilty because she can't stop the cycle of procrastination. Guilt is like quicksand. Once we are sucked into it, our efforts to escape weaken us, and we sink even further down into its muck.

• Missed Opportunities

Phil lost out on the opportunity to enjoy a nice tax refund. Procrastinators could make a list (if they ever got around to it) of all the things they missed out on because they were too busy putting off the inevitable. Casey started her term paper the day the assignment was given, while Jane waited until the day before it was due to begin. While Jane was sweating it out at the last minute, Casey was enjoying a party to which they'd both been invited. A frazzled Jane missed out on the fun. Procrastinators also miss out on much more significant opportunities, like job promotions, the completion of degrees, important relationships, and realized potential.

• Strained Relationships

Procrastination affects not just the one who puts things off, but the people who live and work with the procrastinator. Spouses get frustrated with each other over unfinished projects or goals that are dreamed about but never realized. Parents of procrastinating children battle with their offspring. Children get defensive and rebellious and parents resort to nagging and threats, and before long an all-out war is raging. When the shoe is on the other foot, sometimes children suffer because of their parent's procrastination. They may miss out on opportunities because the parent neglects to meet deadlines or plan adequately for activities and social events.

• Self-Confidence Erosion

DID YOU KNOW?

St. Expeditus is the patron saint of procrastination. Paintings of him found in Germany show that he bears the word "hodie"—Latin for "today"—and is stepping on a crow which is crying "cras"—Latin for "tomorrow." Like several other saints, he may have never actually existed, but instead was the result of a scribe's spelling error, perhaps made in haste, which only adds to the irony of the tale.

It's hard to feel good about yourself when you are caught in a cycle of negative behavior. The unfinished projects and unrealized goals stare at the procrastinator and taunt him. They cause him to feel like a failure as the procrastination cycle continues. And the next time a project, chore, or goal sits before him, a fledgling self-confidence doesn't offer much incentive to change the behavior. The writer and self-help guru Scott Peck says this: "Until you value yourself, you will not value your time. Until you value your time, you will not do anything with it." Procrastinators tend to submerge

CASE STUDY:

Director **John Huston** finished editing *The African Queen* only days before its public premiere in 1951. His procrastination continued, and in 1952 he completed the final cut of *Moulin Rouge* only hours before its December 1952 debut. The film had to be completed by the end of the year to be eligible for that year's Oscar.

themselves deeper into low self-esteem every time they put off a project.

• Sinking Deeper into the Problem

Every time we delay or simply never get started on a project or goal, we sink deeper into the grip of the habit. Psychologists classify a habit as any action that we have performed so often that it becomes an almost involuntary response. The more we procrastinate, the less we can recognize what it is we are actually doing. Putting off those tasks, projects, and goals becomes a kind of second nature. The habit continues and the procrastinator is almost oblivious to his own destructive behavior.

If you are a procrastinator, you are aware of the negative consequences—you're probably experiencing one or more of those right now. And unfortunately, the effects

of those consequences perpetuate the problem. Low self-esteem and guilt sap motivation. Anxiety can lead to poor health and a loss of energy. When coworkers and peers lose trust in you, it becomes harder to trust yourself. And when the dizzying cycle of procrastination persists, it becomes harder to recognize as a bad behavior that needs elimination.

Obviously, these consequences can become over-whelming. The remainder of this book will focus on overcoming the problem of procrastination by putting into place attitudes and actions that counteract the negative behavior of putting things off.

PERSONAL REFLECTION:

Look at the negative consequences you wrote down in Chapter 1. After reading this chapter, do you have any additions to your list? How would your life be different if you did not have to live with these consequences? What are the consequences of procrastination costing you?

☑ *YOUR TO DO LIST:*

List the positive consequences for completing the project you have chosen in Chapter 1. Then list the negative consequences that will result if you do not begin or complete the project, task, or goal. Put the two lists side by side as you continue to work toward the completion of it.

FOR FURTHER STUDY:

Get Out of Your Own Way: Overcoming Self-Defeating Behavior
   —by Mark Goulston and Philip Goldberg

Your Own Worst Enemy: Breaking the Habit of Adult Underachievement
   —by Ken Christian

A Primer in Goal-Setting

---

*What you get by achieving your goals
is not as important as what you become
by achieving your goals.*

—ZIG ZIGLAR

POWER STATEMENT:

> Setting goals helps
> procrastinators clearly see
> where they are headed and
> gives them a vision of how
> to get there.

Kevin received a beautiful leather-bound planner for Christmas. His wife, Molly, had purchased it from a company that promised miraculous results, so she made her husband promise that he would use it. "You bet I will!" he replied, his eyes gleaming as he held the planner and felt its smooth cowhide leather beneath his fingers. Molly was skeptical, but hopeful.

Ever since they had started dating twelve years earlier, Kevin had been a chronic procrastinator. He accumulated unfinished projects around the house, and worse, his career path had been derailed several times because of his penchant for putting things off and leaving important projects unfinished. He had all kinds of dreams and goals in his head—and that's where they had stayed for all those years. Molly hoped the planner would finally get him on the right track.

In March, Molly found the planner beneath a stack of papers. It had been neatly filled out for the first two weeks. The page for goals had been completed and the to-do lists had little checks beside each entry. But the rest of the pages were blank. With a sigh, Molly dropped it in the box she was taking to the donation center later that day.

If you procrastinate, then you probably love the idea of planning and goal-setting. It's exhilarating to think about all the things you would like to achieve and daydream about the big plans that have been swirling around in your head. It's also a safe exercise because it doesn't involve actual work. Kevin really liked to set goals and write them down, but his goal-setting was vague and didn't give him much incentive or inspiration to actually follow through. He'd written down, for example, that he would like to start a Saturday morning golf clinic for low-income kids in the neighborhood where he worked. But that goal stayed in his leather-bound planner, nothing more than an abstract idea.

Like Kevin, maybe you're the type who can dream the dreams, set the goals, and make the lists—it's carrying out all those well-laid plans that gets lost in the shuffle of procrastination. Even fancy leather-bound planners don't make a difference unless you determine to engage in serious behavior modification.

There are several important things to consider when you are setting goals. Any competitive runner will tell you that she spends hours practicing the start of the race— waiting patiently for the gun to sound, pushing off from the start block, and gaining adequate momentum to get through those critical first several steps. The way you start the race is as important as how you finish it. Setting goals is the start of the race. Along the way, you'll face the temptation to quit and old habits will rise to the surface, but if you are careful and intentional about goal-setting, you can avoid the pitfalls and cross the finish line with success.

Principle One: Work on one goal at a time.

As you seek to break the procrastination cycle, don't try to multi-task. Choose only one goal at a time to work on. Procrastinators love to set many goals because setting the goal is the easy part. Resist the temptation and narrow your goals down to one in particular. If you get the urge to set another goal, squelch it. Jot down the idea, put it in a drawer, and don't open the drawer until you have met the first goal.

Principle Two: Start small.

Don't choose a goal that is magnanimous. Deciding to write that five-hundred page novel you've been thinking about is probably not the best place to start if you're attempting to end the procrastination habit. Begin with a small goal like cleaning out the hall closet or organizing the storage shed. These may sound like goals that are hardly worth setting, but success will propel you toward larger goals. Once you have set a goal and fulfilled it, you will have achieved a level of self-confidence that will allow you to move on to a larger goal.

Principle Three: Be specific.

Procrastinators are big dreamers, and sometimes those dreams can sound awfully vague. "I'm going to be more responsible at work," sounds like a good goal until you try and identify what that means. It's too general and formless. You may genuinely want to be more responsible at work, but if you are going to formulate a goal around it, you must bring it into focus. "I'm going to get all my reports in before the deadline," makes the goal visible. Now you have something specific to work toward and you can move forward with steps toward attaining the goal.

Principle Four: Break it down.

Most of the time, working toward one goal means breaking it into smaller goals. Experts call this "de-lumping." (Chapter 9 deals with this concept in detail.) If you want to get all your reports in before the deadline, then you will have to create a series of smaller goals that will ensure that you meet the main goal. These will need to be documented thoroughly, then checked off your list as they are met. Breaking the goal into small bits makes the process less intimidating, and gives you a specific place to start.

Principle Five: Tell someone who knows you well about your goal and get their feedback.

Sometimes we are not the best judge of our good intentions. A trusted friend, partner, or co-worker can look at our goal objectively and offer feedback on whether we are on the right track. If you have set a goal of earning your pilot's license, a good friend might remind you that you get airsick during landing and perhaps learning to fly a plane is not the best goal for you. Your husband might also suggest that before you set the goal of paying all your bills on time, you should set a goal for cleaning out and organizing the file drawer that you throw all the bills into. Make sure the person who evaluates your goal knows you well enough to be honest. They should also have your best interest at heart and want to see you succeed.

Principle Six: Don't be afraid to start.

FAST FACTS:

According to psychologists, achieving a goal you've set produces dopamine, a neurotransmitter responsible for feelings of pleasure. Reciprocally, dopamine activates neural circuitry that makes you eager to pursue new challenges.

Procrastinators set many goals, but often never get past that first step. There are many reasons for this, some of which will be discussed in the following chapters. Although it sounds like a painfully obvious statement, after you set a goal, you must immediately start the process of meeting that goal. Mark Twain once said, "If you have to eat a frog, don't look at it for too long." Once the goal is set, don't allow it to get stale while you ponder and procrastinate. Before long, the goal will become nothing more than a good idea, and you will have had time to formulate many excuses for not starting. If your goal is to spend the day purging your home of unneeded items, take the first step and gather the boxes from the attic. It's a small step, but it sets you on the road to meeting your goal.

You might argue that you been successful in the past at setting and meeting goals, and this may be true. Many procrastinators have met their goals. Consider the student who wrote the paper and turned it in at the last possible moment, or the person who finished their Christmas shopping at the stroke of midnight on Christmas Eve (taking advantage of those all-night drugstores).

FAST FACTS:

According to *USA Today*, the top five things people put off until the last minute are:

1. House chores/yard work—47 percent

2. Holiday gift shopping—43 percent

3. Making doctor/dentist appointments—35 percent

4. Calling relatives—31 percent

5. Changing oil in the car—29 percent

But you'll probably also admit that most of the time, between the setting and achieving of goals, you experienced moments of sheer agony. You hemmed and hawed and came up with a multitude of reasons to start tomorrow. Your peers worried that you weren't going to get the job done, and although you claimed to have it all under control, you were living with the anxiety and stress of putting it off. The goal may have been completed, but it didn't produce any change in your behavior. Successful goal-setting brings about successful completion of the goal, and this is what will give you the self-confidence to break out of the procrastination cycle.

Goal-setting is much more than just writing down a lofty idea and hoping for the best. Rather, it involves careful and thoughtful planning, and it forces you to be realistic about what you can achieve. When you take the time to learn what is involved in successful, effective goal-setting, you have laid the groundwork for successful completion of your goal. And once you have completed a goal with the ease of one who doesn't procrastinate, you will have the self-confidence to set— and achieve—your next goal.

DID YOU KNOW?

Goal setting was a part of ancient cultures, such as the ancient Peruvians who drew out their goals in symbols and paint them in primitive colors on the walls of caves. The Egyptians used to create elaborate rituals to take them from the state of desire to actualization. They wrote out their dreams in advance, believing this would assure a positive outcome.[1]

PERSONAL REFLECTION:

What is your "stopping place" when it comes to meeting your goals, or at what point do you find yourself stuck in the rut of procrastination? Do you have certain goals that you have set many times and never met?

☑ YOUR TO DO LIST:

Evaluate the project you identified from Chapter 1 according to the goal-setting tips in this chapter. If you need to make adjustments, do that now. Show your goal to someone you trust for their feedback.

FOR FURTHER STUDY:

The Ten Commandments of Goal Setting: Violate Them at Your Own Risk!
　　—by Gary Ryan Blair

How to Get Out of Your Own Way: A Step-by-Step Guide for Identifying and Achieving Your Goals
　　—by Daniel G. Amen, M.D.

CHAPTER 5

The Paralyzing Problem of Perfectionism

I think perfectionism is based on the obsessive belief that if you run carefully enough, hitting each stepping-stone just right, you won't have to die. The truth is that you will die anyway and that a lot of people who aren't even looking at their feet are going to do a whole lot better than you, and have a lot more fun while they're doing it.

ANNE LAMOTT

POWER STATEMENT:

Many people fear starting or finishing a job because it may turn out less than perfect, and so they never get started or they fail to finish.

You've decided on a goal, written it out, and determined that this time you will meet the goal without allowing procrastination to creep in. It feels right, until you realize that once again you can't seem to get started. Something is holding you back. You have identified the first step to achieving your goal, but can't seem to take it. In the back of your mind is a nagging thought that your performance might not be flawless.

Perfectionism is a plague that affects many procrastinators, causing their goals and efforts to get stuck in a kind of limbo. Michelle, a chronic procrastinator, scoffed at the idea that she was a perfectionist. In trying to overcome the procrastination behaviors that were making life so difficult for her and those around her, she began seeing a therapist. When he suggested the idea that her perfectionism might be the root cause of her procrastination, she couldn't see the connection.

"I procrastinate about everything," Michelle said. "My apartment is a wreck, I lose all kinds of paperwork, and I have a photography assignment for school due in two days that I haven't even started. How could I possibly be a perfectionist?"

As Michelle talked with her therapist through several successive visits, she began to connect the dots between perfectionism and procrastination. When she thought about the photography assignment that she couldn't seem to get started on, the picture became clear. Here's what Michelle learned about how her perfectionist personality was causing her procrastination behavior[1]:

- **Many perfectionists have a fear of failure.**

Somewhere along the way, Michelle internalized the belief that her self-worth was based on her performance. Richard Beery, a psychologist at the University of California at Berkeley, discovered that those who fear failure equate who they are with how well they perform. Self -worth hinges on ability, and ability hinges on performance. This risky assumption causes people like Michelle to believe that if they fail in their performance, they have failed as a person. Everything they do must be done perfectly. Procrastination is a protective barrier that the perfectionist puts up in order to avoid failure. If Michelle receives a poor grade on her photography assignment, she can blame it on the fact that she didn't give it her best effort.

For the perfectionist, everything is about preserving self-worth, and procrastination is just a means to that end. Michelle began to realize the fear that was underlying her behavior.

- **Perfectionists often adopt an all-or-nothing mentality.**

Perfectionists, because they deeply fear failure, often cannot conceive of imperfect outcomes. For Michelle, receiving a B or C on her photography assignment after she had given it her best effort was a frightening thought. Considering that her self-worth was wrapped up in her performance, her fears are understandable. A mediocre grade would brand her a mediocre person—at least in her own mind.

Michelle began to see that she had a problem with perspective. When asked if she would apply that same standard to her best friend, she was quick to say no. Her view of herself was based on unrealistic expectations. Anything less than perfect was unacceptable.

- **Some perfectionists believe success should be effortless.**

Perfectionists don't like to think of themselves as the kind of person who has to struggle and strive to get a good grade or achieve a positive outcome. After all, if you have to work that hard, it must mean that you aren't smart or capable. Even if her performance was flawless, the fact that she had to work hard to get it that way somehow negated the whole process.

Michelle was frustrated that one of her graduate classes

was difficult for her. "If I was a smarter, I would be able to breeze through it," she said. Because the class required long hours of studying and research, Michelle was once again paralyzed. It never crossed her mind that most everyone else in the class was putting in the long hours and struggling to understand the difficult concepts that were presented. Michelle, in her quest for perfection, didn't like the idea that anything should be hard for her.

- **Sometimes we hold ourselves to impossibly high standards because of a fear of disapproval.**

Ever since she could remember, Michelle had been afraid that she would disappoint someone. Since she was a child, the voices of her parents had reverberated in her memory: "If something is worth doing, it's worth doing right," and "Give it your best or don't do it at all." What was meant to be encouragement was twisted into the message that a mediocre job was unacceptable. Michelle had continued that subconscious belief into adulthood.

Psychologists Jane Burka and Lenora Yuen have found that for many perfectionist procrastinators, their behavior has roots in childhood.[2] Outstanding performance was the means for gaining acceptance, approval, and in the child's mind, love. Second best was not an option.

Michelle continued to hear those voices, and so she set

impossibly high standards for herself. Her fear of disapproval, however, kept her from doing much of anything, which only caused her self-esteem to plummet even further.

- **Some procrastinating behaviors have their root in a fear of losing.**

Burka and Yuen also found that perfectionist procrastinators hate to lose. Although on the surface they may seem to be anything but competitive, the thought of losing is so frightening that they take themselves out of the competition by never getting started in the first place. You can't lose if you never get into the race.

Michelle recognized this fear immediately. In high school she always talked about trying out for the drill team, but she never did it because she was too afraid she might not make it. It was easier to never know than to take the chance and risk not making the team.

DID YOU KNOW?

Perfectionists often procrastinate because they fear making a mistake. Thomas Edison is said to have had 1,600 experiments fail before he successfully invented the light bulb. He said of his numerous failures, "I am accomplishing something. I've found 1,600 ways it doesn't work!"

The perfectionist mindset is so deeply ingrained that it is often hard to recognize and difficult to overcome. Procrastinators don't think of themselves as perfectionists, so they are surprised to find that perfectionism is what is prohibiting them from getting things done. Michelle put in place a few coping strategies to help her counteract her perfectionist tendencies—and get on with life. They might be just what you need too.

• **Be realistic.**

Michelle needed to lower her standards for herself and realize that imperfect results did not brand her as a failure. She also learned to set goals that were realistic and attainable. She decided

> **FAST FACTS:**
> A firstborn child has more propensities toward perfectionism, according to psychologist Kevin Leman in *The New Birth Order Book.*

that instead of setting the goal of making straight A's in graduate school, she would set the goal of doing her best on each paper, project, and exam. She wrote out specific steps toward reaching this more realistic goal.

• **Stop negative self-talk.**

Michelle had a subtle, internal voice that whispered gentle reminders of her failures and weaknesses. Her own self-criticism kept her from taking risks and trying new things, and it perpetuated her procrastination. Each time she was tempted to make a negative statement ("My photography isn't that good, so I'll just finish the assignment and not apply to enter the exhibit"), she turned it into a positive one ("I'll go ahead and apply. It's not the end of the world if I don't make it in, and I may learn something about what I need to do to improve.") Michelle also began reminding herself that there was really no such thing as perfection. Every performance has a small flaw, even if no one notices it.

- **Ask yourself, "What's the worst that could happen?"**

Michelle learned to ask herself this question and give a realistic answer. In most cases, the true scenario was not as bad as she had made it out to be. In the case of the photography assignment that she couldn't seem to start, she realized that making a B or C was not a tragedy. If she began the project and enjoyed it, there was merit in the endeavor. Whatever grade she received would not end her graduate school career.

- **Learn to deal with criticism.**

Making mistakes is part of life. Michelle reminded herself of this every time she received criticism. She determined that she would allow herself to learn from the criticism, rather than fear it. She learned to separate her self-worth from the criticism. When someone pointed out a mistake or a flaw, she understood that they were directing it toward her work—not her as a person. This made a big difference in how she received the critical comments; instead of allowing it to damage her self-worth, she learned to look at it as way to improve her skills and

CASE STUDY:

Susan and Allen represent two types of people: healthy strivers, and perfectionist/procrastinators. Allen has a looming fear of failure each time he is presented with a project or task. He worries about the end results and what people will think of him if he fails. He sets goals that are unrealistic and because anything less would be imperfect, and imperfect is unacceptable. He views his mistakes as evidence of his unworthiness and gets defensive when he is criticized.

Susan is motivated by the pursuit of success and focuses on enjoying the project she is working on. She sets realistic and attainable goals because she knows her limits. She is not afraid of mistakes or constructive criticism, but sees them as opportunities for growth. She gets moving on projects because she knows that the outcome of her efforts is not the measure of her self-worth.

knowledge. The person who never makes a mistake probably isn't doing anything, and so Michelle always remembered to give herself credit for at least having the fortitude to try.

Michelle continued to battle her perfectionism, and she was still tempted to procrastinate in order to keep from feeling like a failure. But with each successful stride toward overcoming both the perfectionism and the procrastination, she gained confidence and a more realistic view of her abilities, performance, and self-worth.

PERSONAL REFLECTION:

What are you putting off right now? What are the fears that are causing you procrastinate? Do you see perfectionist tendencies in yourself?

YOUR TO DO LIST:

List your perfectionist tendencies. Then think of a project, goal, or job that you are afraid to pursue. Write out the worst-case scenario if the outcome is less than perfect.

FOR FURTHER STUDY:

When Perfect Isn't Good Enough: Strategies for Coping with Perfectionism
—by Martin M. Antony and Richard P. Swinson.

Perfecting Ourselves to Death: The Pursuit of Excellence and The Perils of Perfectionism
—by Richard Winter

CHAPTER 6

The Scary Side of Success

Procrastination is the fear of success.
People procrastinate because they are afraid
of the success that they know will result if they
move ahead now. Because success is heavy and
carries a responsibility with it, it is
much easier to procrastinate and live on the
"someday I'll" philosophy.

DENIS WAITLEY

POWER STATEMENT:

Some procrastinators suffer
from a fear of success,
which keeps them from
moving ahead in life.

As we learned in the previous chapter, the perfectionist has a fear of losing that causes him to procrastinate. On the other side of the spectrum, another type of procrastinator has a fear of winning. This person will use procrastination as a means of protection against success. He may set goals and appear as though he desires to meet those goals, but he has an underlying fear that if he succeeds, something terrible will happen.

People who fear success tend to be more content with their procrastination. Take the case of Matt. Unlike Michelle, Matt wasn't really looking to delve into his procrastination issues, but his boss noticed how Matt continually sabotaged his own career advancements, and so he decided to get to the root of the problem.

For several months, Matt had been up for a promotion, but his boss noticed that he'd missed turning in several sales reports and had called in sick to work more than usual. He was often late for sales meetings, and several of his clients reported that he had never showed up for scheduled appointments. Matt's work ethic had taken a turn for the worse, and his boss wanted an explanation. The two were on good terms and after several successive meetings, Matt finally admitted that he wasn't so excited about the idea of a promotion after all.

"I'm not sure I want the expectations that will come

with the new job," he said. "I kind of like things the way they are."

It seems like success should be at the top of everyone's list. Who doesn't want to advance in their career or graduate with top honors or have the respect of their peers for a job well done? For many people, though, success brings with it a host of issues that they would rather not face.

Matt was afraid that more would be expected of him if he was promoted. But there are several other reasons why some people fear success and procrastinate to make sure they don't achieve it.

• Relationship Conflict

There are some people in our lives who can be affected by our good fortune in a negative way. Lifelong friends Ann and Lori owned a catering business together. When Lori had a baby, she sold her half of the business to Ann, who carried on and did quite well. The catering service continued to grow, despite Ann's fears that the business just wouldn't be the same without Lori. She had voiced these fears to Lori, and they had both agreed that they were a good team.

But before too long, it became apparent that the business was actually doing better than when Lori had been a partner, and Ann began to feel uneasy. She knew

Lori was aware of her solo success, and soon she began to slack off on her usual professionalism. She lost some orders and angered some clients. She even began to put off preparing for a catering job until it was almost too late. The business began to fail. Subconsciously, Ann had been procrastinating and doing a less-than-stellar job because she perceived that her relationship with her best friend was in jeopardy.

Ann did not realize that Lori was pulling for her all along, and in fact *wanted* Ann to succeed. Often the procrastinator who fears success does not give enough credit to those friends, co-workers, or family members she's trying to protect.

Of course, there are times when other people may be jealous or angered by someone else's success. These are the times when the procrastinator must be willing to overcome his own destructive behavior and choose not to burden himself by worrying about the reactions of others. If Lori had been bitter about the success of the business without her, it would have been up to Ann to continue with her goals and dreams and communicate to Lori that this was no reflection on their friendship.

• Feelings of Unworthiness

Some people don't feel they deserve success. The boy who survived college by the skin of his teeth may not feel like he deserves that promotion and the plush corner office. The woman who never went to college may not feel worthy of making more money than her college-graduate sister who works as a schoolteacher. These people prefer to keep themselves from advancing in life and use procrastination as a roadblock.

Will had been a problem for his parents from the moment he entered adolescence. He skipped school and partied and ended up living at home with his parents until he was almost thirty. Finally, with the help of a friend, he landed a good job selling hospital equipment. From the beginning, he didn't feel as though he deserved such a lucky break, despite the fact that his parents were ecstatic. He lamented his wasted young adult years, and felt that someone like him wasn't meant for success. He kept waiting for the other shoe to drop, but instead, he just kept advancing in his job.

As the years went by, Will did everything he could to stall his advancement. He believed he deserved only so much, and so he didn't keep rising in the company like his parents and boss had hoped. He didn't allow himself to dream big dreams or make plans to better himself. He stayed at the same level in his job—and in his life.

• Fear of What Success Might Bring

Sometimes success brings about great change, and

there are many people who would prefer not to live with those changes. A friend told Greta that if she would write a book about her experiences as a relief aid worker in India, then he would help her get it published. Greta wanted to write the book and share her experiences with people who might never visit India. She had been an English major in college, so she knew she had the ability to write the book. Greta thought it was an intriguing idea, but she wasn't sure that she wanted to be in the spotlight. What if people criticized her work or took advantage of her in some way? And what if she was expected to write another book and couldn't do it? Greta began to visualize all kinds of frightening scenarios, and so never did get around to writing the book.

> **FAST FACTS:**
>
> Recent studies show that 85 percent of all that we worry about never happens.

Fear of success has caused many people to sideline their goals and dreams, but much of what they fear involves their own skewed perspective of reality. Will, who didn't feel as though he deserved success, believed that he was an unworthy person because of his past actions. But his procrastination was causing his career to be on the skids, which could cause him to lose his job and be back where he started—living at home with his parents.

He had the opportunity to make up for the grief he caused his family, but he was throwing the opportunity away.

Greta also had an unrealistic outlook about her success. She felt as if negative things would begin to occur if she was successful and so she made sure that it didn't happen. But Greta had control over whether she wrote more than one book. And she had control over her response to criticism. She just didn't realize that she had control, and so she had a dim—and twisted—view of success.

Many people who procrastinate believe that they must choose between happiness and success. They are unconvinced that they can have both.

DID YOU KNOW?

Studies indicate that women fear success more than men, although these studies also indicate that women think more about the negative consequences of success before they become successful.[1]

A psychologist who was discussing fear of success with a group of graduate students asked them to think about someone they knew who was always getting things done on time and was very organized. He asked the students if they thought these people were unhappy, or didn't have much of a life. The answer was obvious. People who are moving along in life with goals and the plans in place to meet those goals tend to be quite content and satisfied with their lives. Most of the time, they are not miserable *because* of their success.

Success can bring about challenges, but the person who determines that he will avoid success will face many more painful challenges. He may feel as if he is protecting himself and creating a safe environment, but most of the time the environment he creates is simply a prison from which he will find it hard to escape. If he can break free, he will realize that success is not frightening, but fulfilling.

PERSONAL REFLECTION:

Can you remember a time when you procrastinated because you feared success? What negative consequences do you associate with success? Is a fear of success keeping you from fulfilling any goals or plans?

✓ YOUR TO DO LIST:

If there is an area of your life where you fear success, complete this exercise:

Set aside ten or fifteen minutes and write down what would happen if you succeeded in your endeavor or opportunity: *If I succeed, then....* Keep writing until you get to the core of what you fear. Now look at your fear and determine whether it is realistic.

FOR FURTHER STUDY:

Overcoming the Fear of Success
    —by Martha Friedman

*Permission to Succeed: Unlocking the Mystery
of Success Anorexia*
    —by Noah St. John

CHAPTER 7

Running to Stand Still

It's easy to decide what you're going to do. The hard thing is figuring out what you're not going to do.

MICHAEL DELL

POWER STATEMENT:

Being involved in too many projects and activities can overwhelm and lead to procrastination.

In our culture, busyness has become a virtue. Doing nothing is equated with laziness or low productivity. If you live life in the slow lane, people get suspicious and wonder if something is wrong. Try this: The next time someone asks, "What have you been up to lately?" answer, "Nothing," and watch their reaction.

Of course, there are people who are taking life too slowly. They lack ambition and motivation and prefer to hang out on the sidelines. When people ask them what they have been up to, their honest answer is, "Nothing." They procrastinate because of reasons outlined in the previous chapters. Their fears prohibit them from realizing their potential and pursuing their goals and dreams. In this chapter, we turn our focus to another type of procrastinator: the wanna-do-it-all, over-committed, project-hopping enthusiast. This person has never met a project she didn't want to start, never had an idea that she was too busy to pursue, never saw a goal she didn't want to meet. She's on the go and staying busy. Unfortunately, she isn't getting anything done because she doesn't stay with anything long enough to complete it. Something better always seems to come along.

Most of the time, the wanna-do-it-all, over-committed, project-hopping enthusiast embraces life with gusto. Like a kid in a candy store, she just can't seem to choose which project to throw herself into—at least for the long haul.

If this is your lifestyle—and the reason why you struggle with procrastination—you are probably already aware of the pitfalls. Living life at a dizzying speed is enough to make you, well, dizzy. Or at least very tired.

The over-doer doesn't usually have the problem of getting started. She loves to start. In fact, that's her problem. Starting is so much more fun than finishing and much easier. Her enthusiasm always motivates her in the beginning. Her eyes light up at the prospect of a new adventure.

Ella is a wanna-do-it-all, over-committed, project-hopping enthusiast. Her New Year's resolution was to slow down, but it's the same one she makes every year. On January 1, she promises herself that she will scale back on her activities, but by February 1 she is back to her overachieving ways.

This year, she began with one project: making a family scrapbook. She bought the supplies, spread everything out on her dining room table, and got to work. As usual, her enthusiasm propelled her forward, and things were going great—until the phone rang. It was her friend Daryl, who asked if she was interested in helping with the costumes for the local summer children's theater. Now *that* sounded like a good time. So she said yes, shoveled her scrapbook supplies into a corner, and covered her dining room table with her sewing machine and material.

Things were moving along, and then her garden club decided to put together a cookbook. The costumes didn't need to be done until April, so she agreed to help. She relocated the costumes and sewing machine and covered her dining room table with recipes and her laptop computer. In March, the costumes had to be given to someone else to finish, and she was behind on the cookbook because she had decided to paint her living room.

Ella was living a life of unfinished projects and goals. She never allowed herself to feel the satisfaction of completion because she was constantly lured into starting something else.

The wanna-do-it-all, over-committed, project-hopping enthusiast is a procrastinator in disguise. Most people would never recognize this as his problem, because he seems to be in perpetual motion—always busy, always running. But his running leaves him standing still because he is not accomplishing anything. He has little to show for all that activity, and soon people begin to recognize that he may be dependable in the beginning, but he rarely sees anything through to completion. This syndrome can be the most detrimental in the workplace, where keeping a job often depends on completing a succession of assigned projects.

If you recognize yourself as an over-committed, project-hopping enthusiast, there are several strategies you can put in place to help put a stop to the chaos.

• **Evaluate each project.**

Not every project suits every person. If you are given a choice what projects or goals to work on, take a realistic look at what you can accomplish. Decide two things: if it is the right time for the project, and if you are the best person to do it. Not all projects are good for all seasons. If it's the holiday season, don't decide you want to refinish all your hardwood floors. And if you hate to make phone calls, don't agree to enlist volunteers for an upcoming fundraiser. You're much more likely to see a project through to completion if you remain enthusiastic about the process, and if the process doesn't suit you, you're likely to burn out.

• **Give a verbal and written commitment that you will finish by a certain date.**

Your chances of sticking with something until it is completed are greater if someone can point back to a verbal agreement. Ella decided she wanted to take charge of her over-doing lifestyle, and so the next time someone enlisted her for a project, she evaluated whether it was the right time and if she was the best person to do it. Then she gave her word. "I'll put together the first newsletter for the garden club," Ella told the club president. "And I'll have it to you by the first week in October." Ella followed up her verbal commitment with an e-mail. The club president had it straight from Ella's lips, as well as in writing.

- **Delegate.**

Over-doers are often not good at asking for help, probably because they can't find the time. Part of the evaluation process should be to determine whether this is something you can do on your own, or whether you will need to delegate. Ella decided that she needed someone who could edit the newsletter for grammar and typos so that she could concentrate on writing and layout. She asked her neighbor, an English teacher, to help out. It made the process of putting the newsletter together easier and helped Ella stick with it.

- **Use the back burner.**

Inevitably, when you are in the middle of a project, something else will come along that looks enticing. While Ella was working on the first newsletter, she got an urge to wallpaper the kitchen. She was walking out the door to the wallpaper store when she remembered her commitment to the garden club president. So Ella took out a piece of paper and wrote down, "Wallpaper the kitchen," then put the paper in a file she had labeled "Future Projects." The file was filled with great ideas and opportunities that had come her way while she was busy with the newsletter. After she was finished with the newsletter, she would sort through the file and choose the next project. It was her way of putting everything besides the newsletter on the back burner, and ensuring that she would finish her project before she started another.

- **Use productive self-talk.**

Sometimes it's good to talk to ourselves. Every time Ella was tempted to abandon the newsletter to start something else, she gently reminded herself that she couldn't successfully handle more than one big project at a time. When we are hopping from one project to another, we are actually using counterproductive self-talk.

Some of what Ella used to tell herself sounded something like this: "I'd really like to put together this cookbook, so I'll work on the costumes next month." All along, Ella knew the truth. She couldn't successfully finish the costumes on her own if she didn't stick with it. After she made the commitment to finish the cookbook, her self-talk sounded more like this: "I'll have plenty of projects to choose from when I have finished this one." "I'll do a better job on this if I'm not pulled in two or three different directions."

By the first week in October, Ella had finished the newsletter, and was ready to dip into her file for the next project to begin. In the meantime, her life had lost its chaotic spin, and she was much more organized.

• **Learn to say no.**

For the procrastinator, no may be the hardest word to force out of the mouth and into the air, but it is important to learn how to say it—and mean it. Many people who put things off have overcommitted themselves and agreed to take on projects when they should have just said no. If you have been a "yes" person all your life, this may be a hard habit to break. It's flattering to be asked to take something on, especially when someone gives you the hard sell: "You're the first person I thought of," or "I can't imagine a better person for the job."

A little more self-talk is in order here. You hear the flattering words, yet you know you really shouldn't listen because you're too overcommitted. Remind yourself that

DID YOU KNOW?

A website devoted to unfinished projects offers to take those incomplete jobs, ideas, and projects and post them for possible sale. The site is designed both for people who have abandoned a project and for those who are looking for a project. One person's unfinished project can be passed along to someone else. You can also post a plea for help with your unfinished project, or if you are really sick and tired of it, just give it away for free.

you can't do it all, and that taking this on may cause you to ultimately disappoint the person if it causes you to procrastinate. Better a no

CASE STUDY:

Samuel Taylor Coleridge, the eighteenth-century poet who wrote "Rime of the Ancient Mariner" and "Kubla Khan" had plans for many poems, but rarely finished them. Publishers were always waiting around for his promised works that never material- ized. Scholars have found many of his works left in fragments, and although the writing is superb, they are unfinished and so have been left in obscurity.

in the beginning than a disappointing missed deadline or a failure to complete the project.

Assuming you have the choice, there are ways to verbalize your no without seeming rude or harsh. "This just isn't a good time for me to take anything else on," is an effective answer, and it just might save your sanity in

FAST FACTS:

Among the industrialized nations, workers in the United States take the least amount of vacation days per year. In fact, the average American takes only 10.2 vacation days per year, compared with 30 days of vacation for the average European.

the long run.

The wanna-do-it-all, over-committed, project-hopping enthusiast must be intentional about the choices he makes. There will always be a temptation to say "yes" to everything that comes his way. In the following chapters, we'll look at several specific methods that all types of procrastinators can use to help them start, stick with it, and finish.

PERSONAL REFLECTION:

Are you involved, by choice, in more than two projects or tasks? If so, how would you evaluate the quality of your work on each of these tasks? Do you anticipate finishing each of these tasks?

☑ YOUR TO DO LIST:

List the projects you have started and left unfinished over the past six months. For each project, make a determination about whether you will finish it or not. If not, mark it off your list. Make a file titled "Future Projects" and file the projects that are left.

FOR FURTHER STUDY:

Time Management from the Inside Out: The Foolproof System for Taking Control of Your Schedule and Your Life
    —by Julie Morgenstern

Beyond Juggling: Rebalancing Your Busy Life
    —by Brooklyn Derr, Kathy Buckner, Dawn Carlson, Kurt Sandholtz

CHAPTER 8

Pen to Paper

I don't wait for moods. You accomplish nothing if you do that. Your mind must know it has got to get down to work.

PEARL S. BUCK

POWER STATEMENT:

Writing down goals, writing a commitment letter, making notes, and journaling about the progress of a project help overcome the temptation to procrastinate.

The perfectionist procrastinator, the success-fearing procrastinator, and the over-doer procrastinator have different reasons for their behavior. By now, you have an understanding of which type of procrastination profile fits you as well as a few tools that can help you begin to overcome these mindsets.

Two additional tools are beneficial for the procrastinator, and they are simple to acquire: pen and paper. It's amazing how these two items can give shape to a formless idea, crystallize your commitment, and document the progress of a project, goal, or dream. Writing something down solidifies it. If you can read it over and over again, then it becomes harder to ignore or abandon it.

Here are some elements of successful use of pen and paper—

• **Writing the goal.**

Lee Iacocca once said, "The discipline of writing something down is the first step toward making it happen." Once you have identified a goal, been assigned a project, or taken on a task, it's time to make a note of it. Actually, you'll be best served when you don't just jot a note, but write out a detailed description of what you want to accomplish along with the benefits of completing it. While the pen is in your hand, you'll also want to write out the obstacles that might impede your success. Once these obstacles are in writing, there's less of a chance they'll get in your way.

Rich had always wanted to get an advanced degree, but the idea had been nothing but an abstract thought floating around his brain for many years. He didn't want to get into the program and then quit after a few months (he's done that kind of thing too many times), so he decided to get serious about how to set and meet his goal. He began by taking his pen and paper and writing out his goal.

> *On January 11, 2006, I will begin the MBA program at the state university. The company will fund my pursuit of a degree, but only if I follow through with it. Therefore, I will complete all the coursework that is involved in earning this degree, and finish in three years.*

These three simple statements encapsulated Rich's goal and brought it into focus. He included a start date and a deadline, which took away the ambiguity of how long it would take to achieve it. Rich could now look at his goal in writing, which made it seem real. Now he needed to list the benefits of achieving his goal, which would be a strong motivator for carrying it out. Rich wrote:

> *This goal will allow me to advance in my company and earn a larger salary. The*

additional degree will also give me more
marketability in the event I have to re-enter the
job market. I will also have the satisfaction of
knowing that I have accomplished something
from start to finish.

To Rich, a lifelong procrastinator, this last sentence was important. It also made him a little nervous. In the back of his mind, he wondered whether he would really be able to do it. Because of his history of starting and quitting, he anticipated that there would be obstacles to overcome. Instead of wringing his hands and worrying about what might possibly keep him from reaching his goal, Rich took up his pen again and put the obstacles in writing:

1. I will have less free time.

2. I will be tempted to put off course
assignments until the last minute, which
will cause me to get poor grades.

3. I will have to take class work with me
when I travel.

Rich then listed how he would deal with each obstacle.

Since I will have less free time, I will make a
point to enjoy the free time that I do have. I
won't waste it worrying about schoolwork, but
instead I will take advantage of the time and
enjoy it.

I will post the due dates of each assignment on the calendar above my desk where I am reminded of them and come up with a schedule that will enable me to work on my projects a little each day.

I will not plan dinners out in the evening when I travel, but instead will set aside time in the hotel room to study.

He thought carefully, knowing it was important to be realistic. By doing this, he hoped to neutralize the obstacles before they had a chance to impede his progress. He also hoped that his goal and the plan to reach it would become so embedded in his brain that procrastination would have no room to sabotage his success.

According to Dr. Tedd Mitchell, medical director of the Wellness Program at Cooper Clinic in Dallas, the easy exercise of writing things down reinforces the information in our brain. It

FAST FACTS:

Only about 5% of the population actually takes the time to write down their goals and dreams.[1]

also serves to jog our memory later. And so, writing out a sketch of our goal and its obstacles is a great first step— but we'll accomplish even more as we take the next step.

• Write a commitment letter.

Rich was now ready to take what he'd already written and write a commitment letter to himself, using his goal outline as the foundation for this next step. His letter looked like this:

Rich,

I commit to starting the MBA program on January 11, 2006, and, barring catastrophic circumstances, finishing it in six semesters. This degree will help me advance with the company and will improve my earning potential, as well as giving me an added advantage in the job market. It will also give me the satisfaction of knowing that I have completed a goal and fulfilled a dream. I will remind myself of these advantages every time I am tempted to quit or procrastinate in any way.

I will meet the obstacles head on. My free time will be quality time. I will begin course assignments the day they are given, and work on them in short, manageable chunks of time. I will take my coursework with me when I travel, and arrange time to study at the end of each day.

I will review and renew this commitment daily.

84

Rich signed and dated the letter, which felt a little strange, but he knew he was on his way to accomplishing something significant and defeating the procrastination that had held him back for so many years.

It's important to remember that you're the one who has decided on the goal, and you're the one who will reap the benefits of achieving the goal. A commitment letter is simply another tool that will help you get there. You have made a promise to yourself, and the promise should be documented in a way that keeps you accountable to...you!

Rich made two copies of his letter, keeping one in his work desk and posting the other over his study desk at home. Each time he was tempted to procrastinate on his schoolwork, or give up, he reread his letter.

The writing process wasn't quite over for Rich. He continued to use his tools of pen and paper while as he worked toward his goal.

- **Journal and make notes on your progress.**

One of the first things Rich purchased after he decided to enter the graduate program was a journal. In the journal, he 1) wrote a little each day about his progress, 2) recorded any additional obstacles that were getting in the way along with ways to overcome them, and 3) listed each week's small goals that moved him toward meeting the main goal of earning his degree. He also used the journal to make lists of what needed to be done each day and week, taking great satisfaction in checking off that list as

CASE STUDY:

When he was 15, **John Goddard** wrote a list of 127 goals and called it "My Life List." Now, nearly six decades later, he has accomplished 109 of the items on his list, chronicling many of his adventures in places like *National Geographic*, *Life*, and *Reader's Digest*. A sampling of some of the goals he's reached include: climbing many of the world's major peaks including the Matterhorn, Ararat, Kilimanjaro, Fiji, Rainier, and the Grand Tetons; learning to speak French, Spanish, and Arabic; exploring the 4,200-mile length of the Nile; following Marco Polo's route through all of the Middle East, Asia, and China; composing music; marrying and having children (he has five children). Says Goddard, "If you really know what you want out of life, it's amazing how opportunities will come to enable you to carry them out."

he accomplished the small goals. At the end of each day, Rich would review the progress he had made and record it in his journal. Reading back over these entries gave him motivation to continue forging ahead to achieve his goal.

After a few months of keeping a journal, Rich was able to identify some procrastination patterns that were causing him to fall behind on some of his coursework. He realized that although he had good intentions of studying on the weekends, he always found several "have-to" chores on Saturday morning that kept him from opening his textbooks. By the time he finished these chores, it was afternoon and he found it hard to sit down in his study area and concentrate. After noticing this pattern, he decided to make a list of weekend chores and create an afternoon schedule for completing the jobs. Keeping the journal helped him notice a negative pattern that was causing him to fall behind on some of his smaller goals and might have derailed his larger goal.

DID YOU KNOW?

Young people who begin setting goals in life often come from families where the importance of goals is emphasized. Children of parents who talk about goals and model goal-setting are more likely to see goals as a necessary part of life.

There's just something motivating about writing down what you intend to do. When you put a goal on paper, you've created a record of it and given yourself powerful ammunition in the battle to overcome procrastination.

PERSONAL REFLECTION:

What benefits can you see from finishing the goal you have chosen? What obstacles do you anticipate along the way? How can you overcome these obstacles?

✔ YOUR TO DO LIST:

Write out your goal. Write yourself a commitment letter that lists the benefits of your goal and the obstacles you anticipate. Then post your goal and commitment letter in a place where they will catch your eye each day.

FOR FURTHER STUDY:

Goal-Setting Forms: Tools to Help You Get Ready, Get Set, and Go for Your Goals
—by Gary Ryan Blair

CHAPTER 9

Small Bits

---

*Motivation is when
your dreams put on work clothes.*

HAL ROACH

POWER STATEMENT:

Breaking the task, project,
or goal into manageable,
smaller pieces will make it
less intimidating and allow
you to see daily and weekly
progress.

Zoe had a problem. Her mother had asked her to give her room a spring cleaning and gather up unwanted clothing and items for a garage sale. After several attempts to dodge the chore, Zoe found herself standing in her doorway, frozen, confused, and trying to stifle the urge to run. Her mother had been asking her to spring clean her room for two weeks, but the project loomed too large for Zoe. She didn't know how—or where—to start. To make matters worse, Zoe's mother was furious. She believed that her daughter was being rebellious in her refusal to begin the job, and her pleasant tone had slowly changed into angry demands.

"You're being lazy and disobedient," her mother said in a tense voice. "And so you're grounded until it gets done." Zoe was trapped. She wasn't going anywhere until the room was clean. Even if she had written down her goal, listed the benefits of achieving it, and penned a commitment letter, she still had a problem.

When Zoe looked at the job to be done, she saw it as a giant lump. Psychologists attribute this procrastination-oriented disorganization to faulty perception. The procrastinator sees the job as an inseparable whole—a lump. Zoe couldn't see a starting place or form a mental picture of how the job could be done. She knew the task at hand: cleaning the room. She knew the benefits: a neater (and better-smelling) room and the freedom to leave the house.

But she still couldn't do it. Zoe needed to "de-lump" the job and divide the task into smaller, manageable goals.

Breaking It Down

According to psychologists Jane Burka and Lenora Yuen, most procrastinators only think about "being there," and don't think in terms of being "en route."[1] They don't anticipate the satisfaction of achieving the small goals, which is a motivator for continuing toward the larger goal. De-lumping also keeps you from looking too far ahead. If the project is a large one, it's easy to get overwhelmed when you look at the big picture. Completing the small goals along the way keeps you focused on what is in front of you at a given moment without getting bogged down in the enormity of it all.

Cliff's new job required that he prepare and write the annual report to the donors of his non-profit agency. He knew he was going to have a problem getting started on this, so he wrote out his goal, its benefits, and the obstacles that might creep in as he was working on this report. His goal was to get it written early so that it could be scrutinized and edited in plenty of time for publication. This was an important project, one he couldn't afford to put off until the last minute.

He stared at his written goal and, like Zoe, felt as if he were looking at a giant lump, with no clear starting place.

If he continued to look at the job with that faulty perception, he might never begin. It was time to break down his goal.

The first benefit for Cliff was an improved *motivation level*. He took some time to write out the smaller goals that he would need to meet in order to get the report written. As he wrote, he began to see that the first few small goals could be easily accomplished and he didn't feel quite so intimidated to begin.

Cliff's small goals looked like this:

1. *Read back through the quarterly reports and make notes.*

2. *Outline the report from the notes.*

3. *Write a rough draft of the report.*

4. *Circulate rough draft to the president and administrator.*

5. *Revise the report according to comments made.*

6. *Give finalized and proofread report to the volunteer PR director for layout and publication.*

Cliff then made a deadline for each small goal. He concentrated on only the first goal and thought about what it would entail, things like pulling out the files and spending an afternoon reading through them, highlighting and jotting down important facts. It didn't sound too bad. With that one small goal in mind, he was ready to get started.

Cliff also found that he was able to *see the project in a realistic light* as soon as he had his small goals written out. What had seemed like a Herculean task now looked possible. Each of the six small tasks was a stepping stone, and taking each small step moved him closer toward finishing the report and achieving his goal.

Breaking the goal into smaller goals also gave Cliff *a sense of accomplishment.* Instead of waiting until the entire project was finished to feel as if he had succeeded, he was able to check the small goals off his list as he completed them. This is important for the procrastinator. Because the procrastinator has experienced past failures in starting and finishing projects, experiencing a feeling of accomplishment—even if it's a small accomplishment— keeps him motivated to continue working.

According to psychologist Dr. Timothy Quek, chronic procrastinators are often mired in frustration and depression. Their self-esteem plummets with each task that never gets started, project that goes unfinished, or goal that is never met.[2] Checking off the small goals that make up a larger goal gives the procrastinator small victories along the way.

The Beauty of Lists

Breaking down your goal into small tasks will involve some list-making. Writing out your tasks by hand kicks your brain into gear, because the process of writing involves both sides of the brain. As you write, the right and left brain are forced to cooperate, and the tasks are embedded in your memory in a way that is not possible when the ideas are simply floating around in your head.

If you are a disorganized procrastinator, don't make your lists on scraps of paper that you might lose. Collect them in a central "depository," a notebook or journal. This also allows you to keep a record of the small tasks for each large goal or project. Cliff kept his lists in a journal. He knew that he would be responsible for next year's annual report, so he had his list for completing the project safely tucked away for future use.

FAST FACTS:

Studies have shown that separated, divorced, or widowed people report higher rates of procrastination than currently married or continuously single people.[3]

The tasks for a large project should be listed in chronological order. If you simply jot down the small tasks in random order, you will be unable to see how the project will progress. This is also called "prioritizing." The first step, especially for the procrastinator, is always the most important step.

Carry your notebook with you and glance at it often throughout the day. If you have multiple projects going (and be careful about having too many projects going at one time!), then keep a separate list for each project on a separate sheet of your notebook paper. Reviewing the steps of your project will help reinforce them in your brain. When you have a clear understanding of what needs to be done and when it needs to be completed, you are less likely to be intimidated by the project as a whole.

DID YOU KNOW?

When we write something down, our brain is three times more likely to retain the information.[4]

Rita Emmett, author of *The Procrastinator's Handbook*, suggests creating a "Portable Project Center" if you are working on something that requires multiple sources of information or papers. Cost estimates, receipts, or notes you've made can be kept in one location. If you have to hunt down papers or thumb through files to work on portions of your project, you've created more reasons to procrastinate. The project center puts everything you need at your fingertips. Emmett suggests buying a folder with pockets and a spiral notebook in the same color so you can keep them together. The folder can be stored inside the notebook when you're not using it. All the paper you need for your project can be stuffed in the notebook or jotted down in the spiral. If you have multiple projects going, you can have multiple project centers.

You can purchase folders that have a clear cover so that you can slip your to-do list—the small goals that move you toward completion of the large goal—into the cover. Each time you see your project folder, you will be looking at the "blueprint" of how you will meet your main goal.

Cliff used a portable project center for his annual report. He jotted down notes in his spiral and kept copies of the drafts in his folder, along with all the other papers he needed for writing the report. His five small goals were always visible on the front of his folder, reminding him of the steps that were moving him toward success. He finished the project a few days ahead of his schedule, and enjoyed the satisfaction of knowing that procrastination never got the upper hand as he worked toward his goal.

PERSONAL REFLECTION:

Do you feel overwhelmed by the projects and jobs that are awaiting your attention? Do you have an organized plan to deal with the various projects that must be completed?

Think of a project that you never completed. Did you see it as one big lump, or did you break it down into small goals?

How do you see the project, task, or goal you have chosen? If you are seeing it as an inseparable whole, is this perception causing you to procrastinate on getting started?

✓ YOUR TO DO LIST:

Take your project and break it down. List the small goals that must be done in order to complete it and give each small goal a deadline.

Begin using an organizational system as you work toward completing your project. You can use a portable project center, a simple spiral notebook, or another type of system that will keep you organized and motivated.

FOR FURTHER STUDY:

The Procrastinator's Handbook: Mastering the Art of Doing it Now
—by Rita Emmett

Write It Down, Make It Happen: Knowing What You Want and Getting It
—by Henriette Anne Klauser

CHAPTER 10

Finding Time

*I recommend you to take care of the minutes,
for hours will take care of themselves.*

PHILIP DORMER STANHOPE

POWER STATEMENT:

A calendar and some
scheduling strategies can
help you learn to manage
and use time more
efficiently.

Time is a precious commodity. Most people never have enough of it, but procrastinators seem to have even less. They play games with time and try to manipulate it. They use it as an excuse and then lament that that they can't find it. They waste it, lose it, and make promises about it. Time and the procrastinator have a torturous relationship. But it doesn't have to be that way.

If you want to get control of your time, the first step is simple: buy a calendar, one that's small enough to carry around with you. Your calendar will become an important line of defense in fending off your procrastination tendencies because it will allow you to see your time. You will schedule your week in such a way that you will not have to wonder how or when you will get something done. You will know how much time is available to you and be able to plan accordingly.

Buy a calendar that you can scribble on and mark up, preferably one that will fit in your purse or briefcase. Don't buy one that is too pretty to use—skip the calendars with photographs of Venice or Pomeranians if you're going to be hesitant to write in them or taint the pages with coffee stains. A simple calendar in a spiral-bound notebook is preferable. Get used to carrying your calendar with you, and referring to it when making decision about projects, tasks, or goals.

Many people who depend on their calendars think of them as the other half of their brain. If they leave home without their calendar, they feel lost and unable to make plans or remember what they are supposed to be doing. Procrastinators are often pulled in many directions, disheveled, unorganized, and trying to figure out a way to get things started—or finished. A calendar can pull all that disorganization together *if* you use it in the most productive way; however, consulting it once a week or only using it when you run across it in a pile of papers won't help you.

A Scheduling Strategy

Once you have a calendar, it's time to make a schedule. Dr. Neil Fiore, a psychologist, suggests a strategy called the "Unschedule."[1] This principle goes like this: The procrastinator who has a tough time getting started needs motivation. Often a project seems overwhelming, and the procrastinator wrongly envisions that all his time will be spent working on it, so he procrastinates. The Unschedule is a reverse psychology method that puts work further down on the priority list.

The Unschedule requires that you fill in the boxes of your calendar first with previously committed times such as meals, sleep, and meetings that you must attend. Then schedule free time, recreation, socializing, and then add health activities such as jogging or swimming. Next, schedule structured events such as doctor's appointments, classes, or commuting time. Your blocks are now filled in with non-work activities and you have a clear picture of how much time is left for working on projects or tasks that you are tempted to put off.

Now it's time to fill in your work on projects or tasks, which you'll log only after you have completed thirty minutes of work. Fiore suggests thinking of the Unschedule as a time clock that you punch in and out each time you work on your project. However, you cannot record your time unless you have completed thirty minutes of uninterrupted work. Then, you reward yourself for getting started! Even if you've only put in thirty minutes, you have accomplished something. Keep a record for the week of how much you worked. It's extremely motivating to see the amount of time that you spent working toward your goal.

Fiore also recommends that you spend thirty minutes working before you engage in any recreation activity or social event. This gives you incentive to work and allows you to play without guilt. You should also leave one full day a week free for recreation or any low-priority chores that you don't dread. This day should be reserved as a period of time during which you are not allowed to work on your project. The purpose is to reinforce the notion that life is meant to be enjoyed and to circumvent the resentment that can build up when there is not enough time for play.

Working in thirty-minute blocks keeps you focused on the small segments, not on the finished product. If you procrastinate, then you probably have a hard time getting started on the projects that are most important. The thirty-minute work principle helps take away the intimidation factor. It's easier to start on something when you can see a quick finish to it. Fiore suggests, however, that you never end your thirty-minute work session with a mental block. If you are stuck or mired in a difficult aspect of the project at the end of the thirty minutes, work through it so that you are not tempted to procrastinate when it comes to starting the next thirty-minute work segment.

Looking Back at the Week

At the end of the week, look at your calendar and evaluate how you did on working toward your goal. You have recorded the time you worked on your project—preferably in thirty-minute blocks—so you should be able to see clearly how you spent your time and whether you made progress in working toward your goal.

You might also see patterns emerging. As Patti was evaluating her calendar for the third week of experimenting with the Unschedule, she noticed that her least productive day was Thursday. This also happened to be the day that she had meetings and conference calls in the morning and a book club meeting at night. She was only able to wedge in a thirty-minute block of work time in the afternoon. At the end of the day on Thursdays, Patti felt like she had backpedaled and found it difficult to gain her momentum back on Friday. She decided that on Thursdays she needed to start her day with a thirty-minute work session so that she didn't feel defeated at the end of the day.

When Zach looked at his week, he noticed that he was more productive than he had ever been before he experimented with the Unschedule. He attributed it to the added leisure and recreation time—since he was placing importance on "play" time and deliber-

FAST FACTS:

There are 10,080 minutes in a week.

ately adding it to his schedule, he wasn't as hesitant to work. At the end of the week, he was able to see distinct progress, which kept him moving forward the next week.

The Unschedule will work differently for each person. Make it a two-week experiment, and then decide if you need to adjust it. If you still find it difficult to get motivated for working on your project, evaluate the time of day you are working. If you are more productive in the morning, schedule your leisure time for the afternoon and the evening. If you are less productive on Saturday, then set aside that day as a non-work day. You may be surprised to find that on a day when a leisure activity gets cancelled, you find yourself using that time slot to fit in a thirty-minute work session!

A Clear Picture of Time

The blocks on the calendar will tell the story of how you spent your time and how you harnessed that time to your best advantage. When you are in control of your schedule, the work you're required to do doesn't seem quite as imposing. You know that at least one day out of each week you will enjoy life and put your work aside, and that each day in between will include moments

DID YOU KNOW?

The mysterious Stonehenge, built over 4,000 years ago, may have been the prehistoric form of a calendar. Although there are no written records, scientists have concluded that its alignments indicate seasonal or celestial events, such as solstices and lunar eclipses. The builders of Stonehenge were using the mammoth structures to determine when these events would occur.

for things that you enjoy (more about the importance of leisure in Chapter 13).

Without a calendar that clearly shows how your time is spent, you are at the mercy of guessing how much time it will take to complete your project. When you can look back and see that your project took five and a half hours, or maybe just one thirty-minute session, time becomes easier to predict.

Olivia wanted to put all her Christmas photos on a CD to give to her father, but had put it off for over a year. She decided to begin the project in one thirty-minute block of time. In that amount of time, she was able to gather all the pictures together and put them in a box next to the computer scanner. Suddenly, she felt as if she was halfway finished with the project she had been dreading for twelve months.

The next day, she was anxious to see how many pictures she could scan in her thirty-minute block. She scanned over half the pictures, and had finished the process by the next day at the end of another thirty minute session. In an hour and a half she had successfully completed something that had taken her a year to get started on. Now she knew that many of the projects she was dreading would probably take less time than she envisioned. She was ready to get started on the next project.

Small Gifts of Time

Your calendar will give you a good estimate of how much time you have, and how you spent that time. But tucked away in most days are little pockets of time that you can't anticipate, and certainly can't schedule in your calendar. These are the moments when you find yourself waiting for a client who's late or on the phone trapped on hold or stuck in your car watching the train creep past you. These moments may feel like a nuisance at the time, robbing you of precious moments when you could be getting something done. Think of these unexpected delays as small gifts of time that you can use for something that you probably don't have scheduled on your calendar. Here are a few ways to use these small gifts of time:

- Carry a colorful manila envelope filled with note cards, assorted greeting cards, stamps, and a small address book. You can catch up on some correspondence while you wait.

- Keep a "must-read" book with you—a book for class, or a self-improvement or work-related title.

- Carry your journal with you and make notes on how your projects are progressing.

- Make a grocery list.

When you find yourself using these small gifts of time to accomplish something instead of fuming about how they are a waste of time, your stress level will decrease and you may find yourself looking forward to the unexpected delays.

PERSONAL REFLECTION:

Do you have a realistic perception of time? Do you frequently misjudge how long it will take you to complete projects or tasks? If you are using a calendar, does it help you evaluate how you are spending your time?

☑ YOUR TO DO LIST:

Begin using a calendar. If you choose to try the Unschedule Method, experiment for two weeks with this scheduling strategy. Evaluate how your scheduling method worked for you. Make adjustments that will allow you to continue on the path toward overcoming procrastination.

Carry several things with you that will enable you to utilize the small gifts of time you are given each day.

FOR FURTHER STUDY:

The Now Habit: A Strategic Program for Overcoming Procrastination and Enjoying Guilt-Free Play
 —by Neil Fiore

The Time Trap: The Classic Book on Time Management
 —by Alec MacKenzie

Time Efficiency Makeover: Own Your Time and Your Life by Conquering Procrastination
 —by Dorothy Breininger and Debby Bitticks

CHAPTER 11

A Carefully Constructed Scene

Have nothing in your houses that you do not know to be useful or believe to be beautiful.

WILLIAM MORRIS

POWER STATEMENT:

The environment you work in has a direct effect on how productive you are and whether you procrastinate.

L et's take a quiz. Find a pencil and clear off your desk (if these two activities take you more than three minutes, this chapter is for you). Check the statements that apply:

☐ I have desk drawers that I am afraid to open.

☐ I spend too much time searching for things (i.e. pencils, important papers, to-do lists).

☐ I'm afraid to throw anything away.

☐ My filing cabinet hasn't been opened in months; in fact, I'm not sure where the key is.

☐ I make a trail through my workspace by repeatedly relocating stacks of papers, junk mail, magazines, and other assorted items.

☐ I can't see the top of my desk.

☐ I am drowning in my own junk.

You might be surprised to learn there is link between procrastination and clutter. An unorganized work space, piled with stacks of papers and clusters of junk, clutters the mind as well as the room. It keeps the procrastinator feeling overwhelmed, not only by the project but by all the junk that must be sifted through just to get to the project. Psychologists have found that our environment affects our mood and peace of mind. When the work environment is orderly and organized, we feel more comfortable and relaxed. Paradoxically, this feeling of relaxation gives us energy. Our productivity is improved because we are not sitting in the midst of clutter and disorganization.

Webster's Dictionary defines clutter this way: "1) a crowded or confused mass or collection; 2) interfering echoes visible on a radar screen caused by reflection from objects other than the target."

As the second definition notes, clutter interferes with our target (our goal) by causing us to focus on the junk around us rather than what we should be doing. It blocks clear thinking and blurs our focus, causing us to lose track of where we are in a project. We put things off because it's easier to step away from the cluttered mess and save the work for another day.

Roger, a grad student working on his doctoral thesis, had a work environment that fueled his procrastination. His apartment was adorned with stacks of magazines and newspapers. He had long since given up on putting his clothes in drawers or the closet—the couch, chairs, and the floor of his bedroom were piled with sweaters and jeans. His computer desk and workspace was awash in research material. His file cabinet drawer was perpetually open because it was stuffed full of paper crammed in unlabeled files. As the clutter continued to build, he found it more difficult to pull his information together so that he could work effectively. He spent about half his time searching for a book or some notes he had made or scrap pieces of paper with important information.

Roger was drowning in his own junk, and his head was spinning. It was becoming harder to focus on his dissertation work. He was starting to procrastinate more as the clutter continued to overtake his environment. It was time for Roger to rescue his work environment so that he could work productively and achieve his goal.

Organization consultants offer several suggestions for creating a work environment that encourages productivity:

- **Don't procrastinate when it comes to clearing the clutter.**

Cynthia Glovinsky, a psychotherapist and professional organizer, says the main cause of clutter is actually the fear of clutter.[1] We all have an aversion to chaos that's wired into our brain chemistry, but when we try to sort through the chaotic clutter that is staring us down, our system overloads and we tend to simply run away from the mess. Procrastinators often procrastinate on taking control of their unorganized environment. They view it as an unpleasant project, and they find reasons to put it off until tomorrow. Instead of thinking of "clutter-busting" as just another project, think of it as an investment.

Organizing your workspace now will allow you to work efficiently later.

- **Make it a priority.**

Decide to create a pleasant work environment, and then set aside an hour or two, a day, or a few days to get the job done. Don't answer the phone and put a "do not disturb sign" on your door. If you can't complete your entire workspace at one time, complete one area and schedule another organizing session for the next day. Think of organizing your workspace as an appointment that you must keep.

- **Use the "three piles" strategy.**

Organizing expert Stephanie Denton suggests dividing your clutter into three categories: "keep," "maybe," and "pitch." Throw away the items in your "pitch" file first, and then make a decision about the "maybe" items. Don't shove them into a corner. This only perpetuates the clutter. If you are one of those people who can't seem to throw anything away, ask yourself these questions as you stare at your "maybe" file:

Can I think of a time and reason I will need this?

If I think I will need it in the future, is there a location it can be stored without becoming clutter?

If you have several "maybe" items that you store, revisit them in six months. If you haven't touched them, toss them.

Carefully evaluate your "keep" pile. If you have moved most of your items into this pile, you need to rethink things. Some

FAST FACTS:

Home storage products have become a $4.36 billion industry.

people have a hard time throwing anything away, even if it's something they'll just never need. If you feel like you're living in a world of clutter, there's a good chance you have too much junk.

Roger realized that his apartment, and most importantly his workspace, included many items that he didn't need: outdated professional journals, borrowed books, endless stacks of paper that needed to be thrown out. It took a great deal of fortitude for Roger to toss these items into the big black trash bag he has designated for his "pitch" file, but he continued to picture what his workspace and his apartment would look like after it was de-cluttered. And he reminded himself that clearing the junk out of his living and work space would clear his head and allow him to work productively on finishing his doctoral thesis. For the items in his apartment that were cluttering up his life—and his mind—Roger labeled a big box "charity" and tossed in old clothes, gifts he didn't want (a vase from

Aunt Maude and a snow globe from an old girlfriend), CDs he no longer listened to, and piles of magazines that he didn't have time to read.

After you have pared down your "keep" file, find a permanent location for these items. Files, plastic bins, photo boxes, crates, and storage systems are effective for keeping your "keep" items from becoming clutter.

In her *Procrastinator's Handbook*, Rita Emmett offers some suggestions for getting rid of that troublesome paper clutter:

- Look over material as soon as it arrives. If it's junk mail, don't even look it over. Toss it.

- Pass those papers that other people can handle on to the appropriate person.

- Recycle paper.

- Feed the wastebasket and realize that the world won't end if you get rid of something.

Once you've cleared out all the things you don't need and found a home for the things you do need, you're well on your way to an inviting workspace.

- **Make your space shine.**

Create a work environment that you will want to enter. If you sit at a desk, make sure the lighting is appropriate.

There is nothing more frustrating or counterproductive than working in a dimly-lit area. Arrange the items around you so that you don't have to contort yourself to get to them. If you file papers often, don't place a file cabinet box under your desk where you have to bend and stretch (and bump your head) every time you need to retrieve a file. Keep calculators, staplers, reference books, rolodex—anything you use frequently—at your fingertips.

DID YOU KNOW?

The average executive wastes six weeks per year looking for misplaced documents.[2]

For household projects, make a separate work area for those jobs that you are tempted to put off. Angie was her family's designated bill-payer, but she tended to procrastinate, and the bills were often late. She found herself writing checks over a cluttered kitchen table while she tried to remember where she had put the stamps.

After several years of chaotic, stressful bill-paying, Angie decided to create a bill-paying center. She purchased a small desk at a garage sale and wedged it into a corner of her kitchen. She put three baskets on top of it to hold the items she needed when paying bills: unpaid bills, stamps, and pens. To make sure it was a space that was extra-pleasant, she put a small framed picture and a tiny silk flower arrangement on her table. A "bill calendar" also sat on top of the desk and she consulted it each morning as she passed by so she would know if there were bills to pay that day. When it was time to pay bills, she simply pulled a chair around from the kitchen table and got to work. Everything she needed was at her fingertips.

If you are addressing invitations to the fundraiser, designate a place that is free of clutter, light a candle, and turn on some music. Your work space should entice you to enter it. You are less likely to procrastinate if you are in an environment that is peaceful and inviting.

PERSONAL REFLECTION:

Is clutter and disorganization interfering with you achieving your goal? Look around you at the clutter in your work environment and living space. Are you hanging on to things that you don't need? If so, why?

☑ YOUR TO DO LIST:

Evaluate your workspace (or workspaces). If clutter and disorganization is causing you to procrastinate, use the "three piles" strategy to create a productive and pleasant work environment.

If you find yourself procrastinating about de-cluttering your work environment (and your life), "de-lump" this project by spending fifteen minutes a day on it.

FOR FURTHER STUDY:

One Thing at a Time: 100 Simple Ways to Live Clutter-Free Everyday
    —by Cynthia Glovinsky

How to Be Organized in Spite of Yourself: Time and Space Management That Works With Your Personal Style
    —by Sunny Schlenger and Roberta Roesch

How to Get Organized Without Resorting to Arson: A Step-by-Step Guide to Clearing Your Desk Without Panic or the Use of Open Flame
    —by Liz Franklin

Make Plans for Fun

Our minds need relaxation and will give way,
unless we mix work with a little play.

MOLIERE

POWER STATEMENT:

Play time is especially
crucial for the procrastinator
in order to maintain energy
and enthusiasm for the
project at hand.

It's a little bit of a paradox that if you want to defeat procrastination, you have to incorporate play into your life. Scientists have found that humans are "hardwired" to play. Somewhere in our genetic code is an instinctual and fundamental need to abandon all our cares and worries even for just a short interlude. Everyone can benefit from play, but if you struggle with procrastination, playtime is even more important for you.

Once you have committed yourself to achieving a goal or finishing a project, the realization of what must be done to follow through can become overwhelming. Even if you "de-lump" the project, the fact remains that you have some work to do. Suddenly you have visions of all work and no play. Your hands begin to sweat and you feel cold chills running down your spine. *I'll never have any time for fun*, you think to yourself, and suddenly you're mentally backing away. No one wants to be shackled to a project or task with no hope for recreation or leisure time.

Andy, who had begun doing some remodeling work on the side, committed to building out an attic area of his sister's house. Andy recognized his tendency to procrastinate, so he set his goal ("build out Katy's attic"), wrote himself a commitment letter, broke the project into small, manageable goals, and determined that he would stick to a schedule.

But then Andy started to wonder when he would fit in his down time. He began to resent the fact that he had committed to the project. The morning that he was supposed to begin, he called his sister and postponed his start time until the afternoon. Some friends had invited him to go fishing. "I'll get started this afternoon," he promised her, but he didn't. It was the next weekend before he showed up.

Andy felt like a failure. "I know I should be working," he thought every time he gave in to his desire to do anything besides work. Instead of enjoying his free time, he was using it as a way to put off what he should have been doing. Andy's mindset was this: first work, then play. He spent most of his time trying to find a way around this because he envisioned himself having so much work to do that he would never be able to fit in leisure and recreation. Andy assumed that the best work ethic was to finish the entire project before he took time off to enjoy life. But this mindset was getting him nowhere.

The Puritan Work Ethic

Americans struggle with the notion of taking time off, says Cindy Aron, professor of history at the University of Virginia. She contends that our distrust of leisure is a remnant of thought from our Puritan ancestors, who disdained play and stressed the virtue of work. We love our leisure time, but we also fear its consequences. For many people, time spent playing is clouded with guilt and a nagging sense that they should be busy doing something productive.

Andy's fishing trip was simply an escape, and he spent the entire time trying to enjoy it while he fought feelings of guilt. He knew that he was doing something he shouldn't. He felt as though he didn't deserve to play until the job was finished, but he didn't want to start the job because he thought he would have to give up leisure time. It was a cycle that kept him in the procrastination mode.

Embracing Play

The Unschedule (see Chapter 10) recognizes the need for play in the life of the procrastinator. In fact, psychologists agree that recreation actually makes us more productive and creative. Dr. Neil Fiore, who created the concept of the Unschedule, says that scheduling play time gives the procrastinator a sense of freedom about his life and enables him to more easily settle into short periods of quality work. If we feel trapped by a project and convinced that we cannot enjoy ourselves until the project is completed, then we are more likely to put it off. Who wants to start something that imprisons us and causes us to miss out on the fun things in life?

Dr. Fiore suggests scheduling the recreation *before* you

schedule work on projects or tasks. The idea sounds counterproductive, but it's simple: You will be more likely to work on your project if you know that you will have time for play. The word *leisure* is actually derived from the Latin word *licere* which means "permission." Giving ourselves permission to enjoy play time releases us from the mindset that we will have to give up leisure for work. For most of us, this is a radical concept. We're afraid that if we start enjoying leisure time, we won't be able to get back to the project at hand, but the exact opposite is true. When we give ourselves time to enjoy life, we are better equipped to get back to work.

Andy purchased a calendar and made out a weekly schedule. He included several blocks of time during the week when he could enjoy some leisure, including an afternoon of Frisbee golf with a neighbor and an evening of playing cards with his roommate. Two nights of the week he scheduled dinner with friends. He then blocked off Sunday morning for fishing. Now he had guaranteed himself time for play.

FAST FACTS:

Workers in the U.S. put in more hours than anyone else in the industrialized world, yet are less efficient with their time than other countries.

Andy was skeptical about the schedule, but he stuck to it for the first week.

Since he wanted to enjoy the leisure time that was blocked off on his calendar, he was motivated to begin working on his sister's attic. He began on Monday, knowing that at 5:00 that afternoon he would be enjoying a game of Frisbee golf. He had "de-lumped" the project so that he knew exactly what he needed to get done that day. With a clearly defined deadline for the day's work and the prospect of play time in the afternoon, Andy found himself working productively and without dread.

He stuck to this schedule for the week, and was surprised to find that he enjoyed his leisure time without guilt. He couldn't remember the last time he had gone fishing without feeling like he should be doing something else. Because he enjoyed his leisure time, he had a fresh and creative outlook on the project. For the next month, Andy continued to treat his leisure time as an appointment that he was determined to keep. Knowing that he only had certain blocks of time that he would be working motivated him to get busy once he was on the job. His sister even commented that she had never seen him work so hard.

The Creative Side of Leisure

Children learn through play. It is, as one researcher suggested, the "working world" of the child. Through play, children soak in cognitive, linguistic, and social skills that are crucial to their development. Amazingly, a game of freeze tag or dress-up helps the child's brain figure out how to get along in a complicated world. Psychologists have determined that it is no different for adults. When we are in a state of intense play, cares and worries vanish, and we feel alive and energized. Play releases a creative energy that helps our brain "relax" so that it can sort through complex problems and find hidden solutions.

Often we procrastinate because we have hit a glitch in our project or because it has become more difficult than we anticipated. Getting away from the task and renewing our physical and mental energy through recreation does wonders for solving problems that appear to have no solution. When we are refreshed and renewed, our motivation level increases. We are able to maneuver around the road-blocks and continue projects when earlier we may have been tempted to procrastinate. During a hike one Saturday, Andy was able to think through a problem with the remodel job that had been confounding him for

DID YOU KNOW?

A Stanford University study that began in the 1920s tracked the longevity of a group of children. Researchers found that those who live the longest were those engaged in frequent play through-out adulthood.

several days. As he trekked back down the mountain, he realized that his guilt-free leisure time had cleared his mind and allowed him to solve the problem.

A Warning about Leisure

In order to get the benefits of leisure, you need to be sure that it is *scheduled* leisure time. If you are using play and recreation as a means of procrastinating, then you won't get much out of it—except continued guilt and an increased anxiety level. Play should be a priority on your calendar, but at the end of each week you should also have a multitude of blocks where you have recorded your work on the project or task at hand. If this is not the case, then you will need to reevaluate your schedule. If you find that you are still procrastinating on your project, make a rule that before each scheduled play time, you will work thirty minutes. You can do anything for thirty minutes, right? And you will have something to anticipate at the end of the work session.

PERSONAL REFLECTION:

What is your favorite leisure activity? How often do you engage in this activity?

Do you feel guilty when you allow yourself down time?

Do you subscribe to the notion that life should be work first, then play?

✓ *YOUR TO DO LIST:*

Identify three of your favorite leisure activities that you have not been allowing yourself to engage in. For two weeks, schedule your favorite leisure activities on your calendar (using the Unschedule method). Record your work time as well and evaluate whether enjoying leisure time made you more productive.

FOR FURTHER STUDY:

Beyond Love and Work: Why Adults Need to Play
    —by Lenore Terr

The Overworked American: The Unexpected Decline of Leisure
    —by Juliet B. Schor

CHAPTER 13

The Buddy System

*Accountability breeds
response-ability.*

—STEPHEN R. COVEY

POWER STATEMENT:

Setting up a support system that will encourage and hold you accountable for your progress will assist you in your efforts to stop procrastinating.

t's true that no man is an island. Going it alone is especially dangerous for the procrastinator because she has all those little white lies—excuses for not getting started or finishing—swirling around in her head: *I work best under pressure. I'm too tired to start this now. This is too hard.* The procrastinator needs a competing voice, one that will push her to get going and then hold her accountable to finish.

If you ever went to sleep-away camp as a kid, you probably remember the "buddy system." It's a simple premise: Everyone pairs up so that if anyone gets in trouble, they will have someone who can pull them out of a jam or call for help. As children, we like the idea of having a buddy who can help us out should something go wrong, but as adults we are often resistant to the notion that we might need help. We want to believe that we can go it alone. But life after summer camp often requires that we continue to employ the buddy system, especially if we are prone to procrastinate.

Asking for Help

Pam wanted to set up a small support system to help her begin and finish a difficult project at work. She had been dreading and putting off the project for several months, and the familiar excuses were wearing thin and leaving her feeling stressed. She'd gone through the steps to begin her project—setting goals, paring down her to-do list, writing out a commitment letter, dividing her project into chunks, organizing her office, and using her calendar to schedule the project—but to make sure she was successful, she knew that she needed some accountability. She also knew that there were certain traits she needed in a person when considering them for the buddy system:

- **Understanding.** Anyone invited to be part of the procrastinator's support system needs to understand the problem of procrastination. Pam needed people who didn't label her as lazy, rebellious, or apathetic, but instead saw her procrastination as a behavior that she wanted to overcome. She didn't need someone who simply admonished her to "get going" or "make a to-do list." She needed people who understood that overcoming procrastination was not that simple.

- **Honesty.** Pam had many friends who wanted to see her succeed, but not all of them were willing to tell her the truth, especially if they thought it might hurt her feelings. Pam needed a friend who was willing to tell her when she was making excuses and wasting time.

- **Perseverance.** It wasn't just an issue of starting her project. Once Pam got started, she would need someone who would stick with her until the project was completed. She had been known to get over halfway finished with a project and then set it aside when the going got tough. She needed someone who wasn't afraid to keep pushing her toward the goal line until she crossed it. She would need someone who could be patient with her and not get easily frustrated with the process of holding her accountable.

- *Encouragement.* Just as Pam needed someone who was unafraid to be brutally honest, she also needed someone who was willing to cheer her on. Everyone needs to hear an encouraging word now and then, and Pam was certain that she would need quite a few of those words as she worked toward her goal. A truly encouraging person doesn't need to spout out empty platitudes, but maintain a level of honesty and be willing to offer genuine encouragement.

- *Availability.* Pam wanted someone who would be willing to work in a parallel way with her. She didn't need a tutor, just someone who would work on their end of the project at the same time. It's much harder to continually walk away from a task if you have someone else in the room who is still busy working. This person is not a babysitter, but someone who genuinely understands that the procras- tinator sometimes needs to be in an environment of other people who are working diligently. This person also needs to resist the temptation to chat. It's easy to

> get distracted from the project if you have
> someone in the room who's willing to help
> you procrastinate by engaging in
> conversation.

Pam didn't find just one person with all of these traits. Instead she enlisted several people who could help get her through the project in different ways. Lucy always seemed to have an encouraging word, and Pete was willing to bring his laptop into her office on certain afternoons so they could work on their respective projects in the same space, a routine he carried through until Pam had completed the project. Camille sympathized with her procrastinating friend, and when she caught Pam roaming the halls, she would ask her to report her progress on the project, and then offer an honest assessment. Together, Pam's "team" was able to help her plow through the project and meet her goal.

Stating Your Intent

Writing a commitment letter to yourself stating that you will complete your goal is important; however, you should also follow it up by stating your intentions to someone who will hold you accountable. Pam communicated clearly to Lucy, Pete, and Camille when she would start and finish her project. It was much more difficult to amble around the office filing papers and straightening picture frames when there were people around to remind her that she had a goal to meet. When you communicate your goal to someone else, you're asking them to help hold you to the commitment you have made.

Checking In

Pam had a standing, daily check-in with Lucy, who was her main accountability partner. Lucy would ask her bluntly if she was working and how things were progressing. If Pam was having a hard time focusing on her project, Lucy would give her the push she needed—either a reminder of her stated intent or the encouragement she needed to continue working. Lucy would often remind Pam to keep her eyes off the big picture and only concentrate on the small goals that she needed to accomplish that day.

Pam knew that each day she would be talking to Lucy and reporting her progress. It made it more difficult to procrastinate when she was assured of this scheduled accountability.

No Rescuing Allowed

The purpose of the buddy system during summer camp was to make sure that someone came to the rescue during an emergency. Sometimes it was the buddy who rescued, and sometimes the buddy called someone else. The buddy system for the procrastinator, on the other hand, doesn't involve any rescuing. If your support system has done their part, and you still wait until the last minute to complete your project, they shouldn't be expected to come in and help you dash to the finish line over the weekend. It may be tempting to think of them as a last-minute fallback plan, but their role is not to save you from failure, but to save you from procrastination. Carrying the ball over the line is ultimately up to you.

DID YOU KNOW?

In ancient Babylonia, King Hammurabi included an anti-procrastination measure into his 283 laws by setting a deadline for registering a complaint.

If you feel tempted to procrastinate, you should feel free to call on your support system to for a pep talk, a firm reminder, or to ask for someone to work alongside you—if for no other reason than to keep you planted in your chair! But their role ends when it comes to bailing you out of the consequences of procrastination.

No Nagging

Pam made sure to let Pete, Camille, and Lucy know that nagging her would do no good. Procrastinators almost never respond well to incessant pleas to "get the job done." The measures they employed to help hold her accountable had to go much further than nagging. By holding her accountable in the ways they agreed upon, they were actually a part of the process that would help her overcome her procrastination behavior. Encouragement, persistence, availability, honesty, and understanding all went hand in hand with the other tools she was putting in place to change her behavior.

Celebrating Together

It's good to have someone whose shoulder you can cry on, but it's even better to have someone who can promise you a good time when you've met your goal. Throughout the project, Camille continued to remind Pam that when it was done, they were going to have a big celebration. As Pam met small goals along the way, she and one of her buddies would enjoy a small reward—coffee one afternoon, a movie one evening. Pam was spurred on by the expectation that at the end of the project, everyone would celebrate together, and she was reminded by her support system that they were counting on it.

Enlisting a support system and asking for help along the way should not be confused with weakness. In fact, if you are taking steps to end your procrastination, you should be applauded. Each step you take is in fact a step of courage and strength.

CASE STUDY:

Douglas Adams, author of *The Hitchhiker's Guide to the Galaxy*, wrote a total of nine books, but was a consummate procrastinator. He drank tea, took baths, and spent days in bed to avoid writing. In order to complete his writing, he often required publishers and editors to lock him in rooms and glower at him until he produced. A friend flew to England and camped out on his doorstep in a desperate attempt to prod him into finishing *Hitchhiker's Guide*.

For years, he had been promising a new novel. His tenth book, *The Salmon of Doubt*, was on his table, but he died on May 11, 2001, before finishing a first draft. There are fragments of the novel, but not enough to piece together a coherent story.

Adams would put off working as long as possible, and then finish projects in a frantic rush. "I love the sound of deadlines as they go whooshing by," he once said.

PERSONAL REFLECTION:

Do you find it difficult to admit to other people that you procrastinate? Does asking for help come easily for you, or do you resist it? How willing are you to allow someone to give you honest feedback, and hold you accountable to commitments you have made?

✓ YOUR TO DO LIST:

Identify some people who could help keep you accountable to meet your goal, and ask them if they would be willing to be a support for you as you work toward the goal.

FOR FURTHER STUDY:

The Procrastination Workbook: Your Personalized Program for Breaking Free from the Patterns That Hold You Back
—by William Knaus

To Do Doing Done
—by G. Lynne Snead and Joyce Wycoff

CHAPTER 14

Backsliding Ahead

Our greatest glory is not in never failing,
but in rising up every time we fail.

—RALPH WALDO EMERSON

POWER STATEMENT:

In order to overcome procrastination, you must accept setbacks and give yourself permission to backslide while maintaining a determination to succeed.

As we have seen in previous chapters, one of the biggest fears of procrastinators is failure. Fear of failure hinders the ability to get started, and once we do, it whispers to us a multitude of tempting reasons to quit. Fear often keeps the procrastinator paralyzed, and it's because of the power of fear that at the beginning of a project, goal, or task, you should accept the possibility that you will fall down a few times before you succeed. You should never plan to backslide, but you should make a plan in case you find yourself tumbling down the hill. Here are a few proactive measures you can take.

- **Give yourself permission to be less than perfect.**

The perfectionist's mindset says that there is no point in doing the job if there's any chance that it will turn out as anything less than a flawless and stellar achievement. For the procrastinator, this perfectionist thinking keeps her in a holding pattern and causes her to quit before she gets started. It also may cause her to believe that she can never overcome her procrastinating behaviors.

A Japanese proverb says, "Fall seven times, stand up eight." Giving yourself permission to fall is an important step in overcoming procrastination. If you've set a goal and put in place all the elements that you feel will help you achieve your goal, you may be tempted to believe one step backward means that you are doomed to never end the procrastination cycle. This is perfectionist thinking at its best—or worst.

Tell yourself that if you fall in your efforts to end procrastination, you'll get right back up and keep going. Jeff wanted to end his habit of studying for tests the night before he took them. His grades reflected a chronic procrastination habit, and he was determined to take the necessary steps to end this behavior.

One week into his efforts, though, he wasted two days that he could have been studying. Instead of opening his textbooks, he accepted some friends' request to help them clean out the garage so their band could use it to practice. Jeff told himself that he was doing a good deed for his friends, and gave himself the usual excuses. Then he realized that he had taken a step back in his efforts to stop procrastinating. He felt like a failure and told himself that this was the proof that he couldn't change.

Jeff had expected that once he had determined to stop procrastinating, it would be smooth sailing. He reasoned that since he had put into effect all the necessary steps for success, failure was impossible. He had set himself up for a hard fall with expectations that were set too high.

- **Learn from your mistakes.**

Often the most valuable lessons we learn are those that come when we make a mistake. When you are attempting to break the procrastination habit, it is inevitable that you will experience setbacks. Instead of dwelling on what you perceive as a failure, look for the lesson in it.

Jeff thought about what had caused him to abandon his commitment to stick with his goal. Only two weeks earlier, he had a plan in hand and was determined to not fall back into the behavior of studying at the last minute. But it had only taken one tempting opportunity to cause him to backslide.

When his buddies asked him to help them prepare a band practice area, Jeff's first thought was, "I can't because I have to study." He realized that most of the time, he procrastinated because he saw goals or projects as something being forced on him. When given the choice between an afternoon helping out some friends and having to study, he chose the activity that was more fun.

He learned a valuable lesson from his backsliding: He needed to view his goal as something that he *wanted* and not an obligation. Jeff decided that the next time he was presented with an opportunity that would cause him to put off studying, he would look at his goal in a different way. Instead of telling himself that he "had" to study, he would remind himself that he "wanted" to form a new study habit, and procrastinating would not help him achieve his goal.

Jeff took the opportunity to see what he could learn from the setback and used it to move forward.

- **Accept your limits.**

The techniques that you have chosen to help overcome procrastination are not all-or-nothing cures. According to psychologist Dr. Robert Simmonds, behavior change is a process composed of many steps. You may have success in dealing with some components of the problem and struggle with others. Most people, he adds, relapse and have setbacks during the process.

Be realistic about how long it may take you to overcome procrastination. Some people may be able to put techniques for overcoming into place and have quicker success than others. If you look at it as a process that contains many steps, then you're less likely to see one setback as an end to the entire process.

- **Remind yourself of what you have accomplished.**

Jeff made small strides, but he reminded himself that he should be proud of those small steps. Even before he encountered setbacks, he had already noticed positive improvement in his study habits. Instead of leaving his books stuffed in his backpack until it was time to cram, he had taken them out and reviewed some of the chapters the same week they were covered in class. Although it was a fairly small improvement, it was *something*. He was certainly further ahead than he had been two weeks ago when he had made the commitment to change his study habits.

FAST FACTS:

Research has found that only about 20 percent of all people who are attempting to change a behavior make a complete change on their first try.[1]

Focusing on the improvements you have made, even if they may not seem so significant, will help you deal with the times that you backslide away from your goal of overcoming procrastination.

• **Forgive yourself and move forward.**

The "poor me" mode is the place where we often get stuck when we have encountered setbacks. It's easy to dwell on our mistakes, our failures, and the things we should have done differently. But staying in this mode will zap the motivation to continue our efforts to change our negative behavior.

When you backslide, give yourself plenty of grace and then get back on track. Be careful that you don't use negative self-talk, which will only sink you further into feelings of failure. Instead of telling yourself that you are a loser and a hopeless procrastinator and a generally terrible person, tell yourself that you are making progress because you have recognized your problem and lined out some steps to overcome it.

Jeff was tempted to sit and wallow in his failure to study a little each day for his exam, but he knew that this would only keep him from standing back up and trying again. Instead of wishing that he had done things differently, he forgave himself and determined that he would continue on the path of becoming a person who had left the procrastination habit behind.

DID YOU KNOW?

One of the earliest written records of the word *procrastination* is found in a copy of a seventeenth-century sermon by a Reverend Anthony Walker. In his sermon, Rev. Walker makes it clear that procrastination is sinful, and that he and other ministers have called on their congregations to rally against it. This view of procrastination as a sin was a new one. Earlier cultures were ambivalent or positive about procrastination. Roman use of the term seemed to reflect the notion that deferred judgment may be necessary and wise when waiting out an enemy or displaying patience in military conflict.

Conrad Hilton says this:"Success seems to be

connected with action. Successful people keep moving. They make mistakes, but they don't quit." When you are backsliding, it doesn't feel like you are moving forward, but if you learn from your mistakes and are able to forgive yourself and forge ahead, you are accomplishing more than you can imagine.

PERSONAL REFLECTION:

Have you accepted the possibility of backsliding as you seek to overcome procrastination? When you encounter setbacks when working toward goals, do you tend to see yourself as a failure? How does that thinking affect your work and your progress toward your goal?

☑ YOUR TO DO LIST:

Write down three things that you tell yourself when you make mistakes. Then write down three things you would tell someone else if they made a mistake. Compare the lists and determine that you will use positive self-talk as you seek to overcome procrastination.

FOR FURTHER STUDY:

Great Failures of the Extremely Successful: Mistakes, Adversity, Failure and Other Stepping Stones to Success
—by Steve Young

Optimal Thinking: How to Be Your Best Self
—by Rosalene Glickman

CHAPTER 15

Rewards Along the Way

Procrastination is the gap between intention and action.

—HARA MARANO

POWER STATEMENT:

Rewards produce motivation and give us an added excitement about continuing and finishing the project.

Even though you have put a program into place to guide you toward your goal, there will be days when you find yourself drifting away from the job to alphabetize your soup cans or clean out your inbox. One key to staying on track is incentive. If you're waiting until you complete your goal to reward yourself for your hard work, you may find your motivation waning at some point before the finish line. Finishing the task will bring the reward of satisfaction, but chances are you will need some positive inspiration between the start and the finish line.

Punishing yourself for procrastinating is not nearly as effective as rewarding yourself for good behavior. Rewards give you something to anticipate and remind you that there are benefits to not procrastinating. Everyone wants to have something to look forward to at the end of a long work session. For the procrastinator, rewards also need to be put in place for the completion of a short work session. The idea is to get *started*. If the knowledge that you will treat yourself to a cup of cappuccino at the end of thirty-minute work session gets you going, then the reward system has done its job. Here are some ideas for using rewards as you move forward with your project.

- **Use the "timeboxing method."**

Steve Pavlina, a personal development coach, suggests selecting a small piece of your task to work on for thirty minutes, then choosing a small reward to give yourself at the end of the work session.

The reward should come immediately after you have finished your thirty minutes of work. Don't promise yourself you'll rent a movie on Friday night if you work for thirty minutes on Friday morning. Choose something small but enjoyable—a walk in the park, a call to a friend, a nap. The important thing is that the reward is enjoyable for you.

Pavlina notes that at the end of a thirty-minute work session, you may decide to keep going on the task at hand. As you continue to work, you know that your reward is waiting for you when you are done, and you have cleared the hurdle of getting started. Suddenly the pressure is off and you can give your full attention to the piece of the project you are working on.

If a thirty-minute work session is too long, shorten it to ten or fifteen minutes. If you tell yourself that you will only work ten minutes before enjoying a small reward, chances are you will work longer.

- **Keep rewards proportional.**

If you have just finished a thirty-minute work session, don't plan a weekend of skiing, and don't shortchange yourself with a scoop of ice cream for months of working to achieve your goal. Your short spurts of work should have corresponding short spurts of rewards. The small goals that move you toward the larger goal may require larger rewards. When you have met your goal and you can claim victory in successfully completing the task or project, a substantial reward is in order. Fran's goal was to trace her family tree and write a concise history based on her research. After she had written out her goal and divided it into four smaller goals, she decided on corresponding rewards for each phase of her work. Her lists looked like this:

30 minutes of work	Small goals obtained	Goal completed
Watch television show	Movie w/ the girls	Weekend at the beach
Root beer float	Afternoon at the museum	
Solitaire on the computer	Day of shopping	
Call and chat w/ Brooke	Dinner theatre with Don	
Power walk		
Nap		
Read a novel chapter		
Swim at the fitness center		

- **Focus on time spent working, not achievements.**

There were plenty of thirty-minute sessions when Fran didn't have much to show for her work, but she rewarded herself for sitting down and making the effort. As long as she didn't goof off and wander out of her chair to straighten the pictures in her office or some other obscure task, she treated herself to one of the small rewards. At other times, once she got started, she stayed engrossed in her work for much longer than thirty minutes. Either way, she knew that at the end of her time, she would be able to engage in an activity that rewarded her for sitting down and sticking to the task.

Rewards increase the probability that the desired behavior will be repeated, which means that even if your thirty minutes was not as productive as you might like, it's likely that you will sit back down again later in the day or tomorrow and get started once again. It bears repeating: *Getting started* is the important thing for the procrastinator.

- **Let others join in on your rewards.**

Fran found that it was even more motivating when someone else was counting on something fun at the end of her work session. When she had a tough time getting motivated to work on her projects (Monday mornings seemed the hardest) she called a friend to invite him or her to participate in whatever reward she had chosen. If her friend Cameron was counting on her to walk with him at noon, Fran knew that she had better make sure she didn't waste her thirty-minute work session. She didn't want to have to call and tell him that she hadn't earned her reward time.

Make sure the person you have planned time with understands why you have set up the reward system. It brings added accountability if a friend can ask you about your work session when you meet. Fran knew that when she and Cameron met at the park, he would want to hear about her progress, so she made sure that she had something good to report while they walked.

- **Don't cheat the system.**

If you goof off for thirty minutes and then reward yourself with a nap, you are less likely to achieve your goal. The reward becomes yet another way to procrastinate, instead of a motivator. Although you control the reward system, you also are in control of whether you cheat that system. It takes a certain amount of willpower to stave off a nap or a café latte until you have fulfilled your promise to work for thirty minutes, especially if no one other than you knows the difference.

FAST FACTS:

In a recent survey of 300 college students who describe themselves as procrastinators, 47 percent said they would rather donate blood than write an assigned paper. Almost one-third would rather visit the dentist, and more than one in five said they would rather pick up trash on campus than get their paper done. [1]

Fran found that when she sat down at the computer to do research, it was tempting to sneak in an e-mail check every now and then. If she had received e-mail, it took some time to read it, and then she always felt the need to respond. Suddenly her thirty-minute work session had been whittled down to ten or fifteen minutes. Even though she had sat at her desk chair for the allotted time, she could not honestly say that she had stuck with the task. She had procrastinated by allowing herself to give in to distraction. She knew that a power walk or a root beer float wasn't justified.

Fran remembered that setbacks are a part of kicking the procrastination habit, so instead of dwelling on her failure to stick with the task, she determined that during her next work session she would start fresh. Once again, she would have the carrot of a reward dangling in front of her.

- **Don't be afraid to give yourself credit.**

The concept of giving yourself a reward may seem a bit self-indulgent. We're not used to the idea that we give something to ourselves, especially something enjoyable like a nap or a favorite dessert. We don't hesitate to reward others for their work, yet we are often uncomfortable applying the same principle to our own work. Think of the reward system as one more stepping stone toward defeating procrastination. Rewards help us associate pleasure with tasks we dread and give us the desire to get started on projects that we might otherwise put off. Rewards remind us that there is something beyond the task before us. When we can begin the task knowing that we have something to anticipate after we complete a mere thirty minutes of work, the task seems less imposing.

PERSONAL REFLECTION:

What motivates you to begin working on a task? Do you give yourself rewards for working, or do you always expect other people to reward you? Are you comfortable with the idea of rewarding yourself?

✓ YOUR TO DO LIST:

Make a list of small activities you enjoy—enjoying a scoop of ice cream, calling a friend, reading a chapter of a good book. Then make a list of more significant activities you enjoy—watching a movie, going to a play, cooking a gourmet dinner for friends. This week, use the small rewards as incentives for doing a small chunk of work and the larger rewards for meeting one of your small goals.

FOR FURTHER STUDY:

The Procrastinator's Success Kit
    —by Alyce Cornyn-Selby

The Tomorrow Trap
    —by Karen Peterson

CHAPTER 16

The Procrastinators Around You

*Tomorrow is the day when idlers work,
and fools reform.*

—EDWARD YOUNG

POWER STATEMENT:

People who live and work
with other procrastinators can
find effective ways to deal
with the people in their lives
who put things off.

Procrastinators can be tough to work with, and even harder to live with. You may have found yourself stifling the urge to scream when your child announces to you at 10 P.M. one evening that he needs computer paper for an essay due tomorrow. If you are an employer, you may be fed up with missed deadlines and employees who hand off projects to other people at the last minute.

If you're the procrastinator, it may be beneficial for you to see how your procrastination habits affect those around you. According to some estimates, procrastination costs our industries millions of dollars in lost work and forces executives to let go of many thousands of employees. In our homes, procrastination causes relationship strife between parents and children, spouses, and extended family members who often must intervene in these battles.

It is important for anyone who lives or works with a procrastinator to understand the causes behind the behavior (see Chapters 5-7). If you are a procrastinator who has to deal with other procrastinators on a daily basis, you will probably be able to understand better than anyone the emotions and anxiety that surround the habit. If you are trying to change your own behaviors, you can use the principles you have learned to encourage and aid the procrastinator in your life.

In the Workplace

- Use lots of positive words.

Procrastinators need encouragement, not criticism. Often, those who have perfectionist tendencies and those who fear success have grown up hearing negative statements about their efforts. Alexis made decent grades in school and excelled in several outside activities. But her father always used negative statements as a way to motivate her, things like, "They won't let you into college just because you can twirl a baton," or "You're not using the car until the B in Chemistry is an A."

Over time, Alexis began to internalize the negative statements and made them her own. She hears the criticism reverberating in her head every time she takes on a project or tries to set a goal. "Let's see how long you'll stick with that," she tells herself, or, "If I screw up this project, they'll never forgive me."

Alexis puts so much pressure on herself to make everything perfect that she has a hard time getting started on anything. Procrastinators need positive statements coming their way. "You need to have this finished by Monday," can be replaced with: "I'm confident you can get this done by Monday." Employers and co-workers don't need to treat procrastinators like children, but they do need to keep in mind that negative statements don't motivate the procrastinator; they only paralyze her even more.

Constructive criticism is often anything but constructive. The statement, "There are all kinds of problems with this report," can be replaced with, "This is a great start on the report. We just need to add in a few more facts and rework the last paragraph."

- Place emphasis on teamwork.

Good leadership always stresses the idea that "we're all in this together." Procrastinators are more likely to feel motivated to start and finish a project if they feel as though someone is in the boat with them. The goal should belong to everyone, even if one person is working on the project. This doesn't mean that the procrastinator gets bailed out by the "team" if he doesn't come through; rather, the objective is to use teamwork to help the procrastinator get past the barrier of not starting. It's a less intimidating work environment if everyone is clearly on the same side.

- Offer choices.

Instead of mandating that an employee have a projected finished by Tuesday—or else—a better approach is to ask whether he can turn it around Monday afternoon or Tuesday by noon. Being presented with a choice gives him discernable control over the deadline. Procrastinators can easily feel backed into a corner by the projects and due dates, which only heightens the desire to put off starting. It feels much better to know that you have chosen the deadline.

Kelly knew that Paul was a procrastinator. In finding ways to help him work efficiently, she found that giving Paul some choices made a difference in his attitude as well. "I'd like for you to do the first draft of the ad campaign," Kelly told Paul. "What do you think your turnaround time would be on that?"

Paul immediately entered into a dialogue with his boss about what he thought was a reasonable deadline. Kelly already had a deadline in mind, but she was willing to compromise a little so that Paul could be brought into the decision-making process. It gave Paul some ownership of the deadline and made it seem less imposing.

In the Home

- Stop Nagging.

There is nothing that will deafen the procrastinator more than hearing someone else nag at her to get the job done. If your daughter has been putting off starting her science fair project, she won't be motivated by a constant and repetitive reminder. She already knows that she needs to get started, and chances are she is hearing the same nagging from her inner voice. She doesn't need a chorus of voices telling her what she already knows. A wife who nags her husband to clean out the gutters will elicit even less of a response.

Suppress the urge to nag, regardless of how strong it may be. If you live with a procrastinator, remind yourself that you will never motivate him to change his behavior by continually reminding him of his failure. And that's how nagging is often interpreted, as a reminder of the procrastinator's shortcomings, and most of the time it goes unheard—and unheeded.

- Allow failure.

Often the most productive lesson for an older child who procrastinates is to allow them to suffer the consequences of their behavior. Instead of nagging your daughter to start her science fair project, give her some tools to help her start (a calendar, help in organizing her workspace, aid in writing her goal, encouragement to de-lump the project) and then step back and let her do the job. Make it clear that you will not bail her out, but that you will be there to offer assistance if she seems to be making an effort. If she still chooses to put it off and risk missing the due date for the project, realize that the lesson she learns by failing may motivate her to start changing her behavior.

- Don't value performance.

It is important to let family members know that you value them, but not because of what they do or how well they do it. Procrastinators are often performance driven, which keeps them fearful of delivering anything less than a flawless performance on any project, task, or job. They need to know that their performance does not define who they are. Family members need to take the time to communicate this. As a parent, you may have to let go of some dreams you had for your kids in order to let them know that you love them in spite of what they do—or don't do.

- Be firm.

Don't let your family member's procrastination drive you back into nagging. If your child or spouse is perpetually running late, causing you to stand by the door dangling the keys and shouting hair-raising threats, you may need to toughen your

FAST FACTS:

According to the research of Dr. Piers Steel, professor at the University of Calgary, in 1978 about 15 percent of the population said they procrastinated somewhat, and one percent said they were chronic procrastinators. In 2002, about 60 percent of the population said they procrastinate somewhat, and six percent said they were chronic procrastinators. [1]

approach. Tell them what time the car will be pulling out of the driveway—and then make sure that you follow through. Count backwards to make it easier for them to plan: "We need to leave at six-thirty, so we better start getting ready about five thirty and have everyone rounded up by six-fifteen." This gives the procrastinator three clear deadlines, making it easier to "de-lump" the goal of leaving at 6:30. If you are the only one in car ready to go at 6:35 (a five-minute grace period is permissible), then away you go. Assuming your spouse can drive, he or she can follow along whenever they are ready. Arriving somewhere alone a few times may cause the procrastinating spouse to rethink the behavior. You should never leave a child behind, but taking away the privilege of attending the event several times may cause him to realize you are serious about helping him learn how to plan ahead to achieve the goal.

- Model getting things done.

If you live or work with a procrastinator, don't expect family members or employees to be motivated if you aren't. If you struggle with procrastination, work on your own behavior before you point the finger at someone else. If you expect others to get projects finished on time, be sure that you don't put things off. But don't think you have to walk around pointing out your ability to get things done and stick with projects, since most of the time people are motivated to imitate positive behavior when they see it, not when they hear about it.

If you are trying to get your children to finish things they've started, don't make a habit of leaving your own projects unfinished. It's hard to convince a child that there is value in completing an assignment if you have had lived for several months with the house half-painted or a garden plot that you've never gotten around to planting. Children are always watching their parents for cues. If you can't back up your words with actions, it's better to stay silent.

- Be encouraging and show grace.

Children need positive words and lots of forgiveness. When your child is taking steps toward ending the procrastination cycle, acknowledge the effort instead of criticizing any weaknesses. If you are dealing with a

CASE STUDY:

Dr. Timothy Pychyl, associate professor of psychology at Carleton University in Ottawa, Canada, has found that children of authoritarian parents are prone to procrastinate. These children postpone choices because their decisions are so frequently criticized, or the decisions are made for them.[2]

spouse or extended family member who procrastinates, the same rule applies. Criticism will never motivate the procrastinator to change his or her behavior, while encouraging words are an amazing catalyst for success. In the end, everyone must take responsibility for his or her own actions and efforts, but having someone cheering from the sidelines can make a big difference.

Karla's parents had made sure that they controlled every aspect of her life. They rarely let her make choices, and after so many years of being under their thumbs, she rebelled. When Karla became an adult, every project or task was equated with the chores she had to do as a child, so she would put things off as a way to satisfy herself that she was finally in control. After several failed careers and ruined relationships, she realized that she was only hurting herself. She found her control by defeating procrastination and finally achieving some goals in her life.

PERSONAL REFLECTION:

Think of three procrastinators you live and work with. How are their habits affecting you? Is procrastination getting in the way of an important relationship? Are you prone to react with anger and criticism?

✓ YOUR TO DO LIST:

If a family member's procrastination is getting in the way of your relationship, talk to them about it and offer to help come up with ways to deal with the behavior. The principles outlined in this book are a good starting place.

FOR FURTHER STUDY:

The Procrastinating Child: A Handbook for Adults to Help Children Stop Putting Things Off
    —by Rita Emmett

Working with Emotional Intelligence
    —by Daniel Goleman

CHAPTER 17

The Freedom of Getting Things Done

*The really happy people are those who have
broken the chains of procrastination,
those who find satisfaction in doing the job
at hand. They're full of eagerness,
zest, and productivity. You can be, too.*

—NORMAN VINCENT PEALE

POWER STATEMENT:

Getting things done gives you
a sense of control over your
life and a feeling of freedom
and confidence.

There's no magic formula for overcoming procrastination. It takes persistence and a determination to keep trying even when it seems as though you aren't getting anywhere. There will many times when you find yourself taking two steps forward and three steps back. You'll worry that procrastination is a part of your genetic makeup and that all methods for overcoming it are beyond your capabilities.

And then one day you'll realize that you have, in fact, made progress. You'll finish a project or meet several of the small goals that move you toward your larger goal. Someone will recognize that you met the deadline and compliment you on your dependability and then you will know that getting things done is within your reach.

Once you have successfully achieved a goal without the flimsy excuses, missed deadlines, and relentless anxiety that accompany procrastination, you won't want to go back. The old way of doing things will seem like a prison that keeps you from enjoying life.

Shackled by Procrastination

Barbara was up until 1 A.M. finishing a project that was supposed to be done two days earlier. She set her alarm for 6:30 A.M., but hit the snooze and slept until 7:30. Now she only had thirty minutes to get to work. She flew through the house, searching for clean clothes and trying to gather up her work papers. She had no time for breakfast (there was no milk anyway, because she had been putting off a trip to the grocery store), and no time to stop and get something to eat. She found half a candy bar in her briefcase and munched on it as she sped to the office. In the middle of the drive, she remembered that she was supposed to set a box of dishes on the porch for a friend to borrow. She had meant to set them out the night before, but had kept putting it off. She fumbled around in her bag for her cell phone so she could call and apologize to her friend, but when she found the phone, the battery was dead. She had meant to charge the battery last night, but left the phone in the car thinking she would do that later.

FAST FACTS:

Psychologists have categorized procrastinators versus those who don't procrastinate in this way: Procrastinators think and act in terms of "wishes and dreams" while non-procrastinators' focus on "oughts and obligations."[1]

By the time Barbara reached her office, she was completely stressed out and unable to focus. She lived her life this way—in a constant state of disarray, anxiety, and guilt. Her house was a mess, projects were scattered everywhere, and she woke up every morning wondering what she had forgotten to do the previous day. She didn't know how long she could continue to live like this. She was imprisoned by procrastination. It was wrecking her health, affecting her relationships, and making her feel worthless. She wanted to be able to breathe and enjoy life. Barbara decided it was time to stop procrastinating and start living.

She realized that she had a hard time starting and finishing projects because she was afraid of failure, so she made a decision to put some tools and methods in place to counteract that fear. She learned how to set goals and how to get started on projects using the de-lumping method, a calendar, and the Unschedule. She organized her office and became deliberate about rewarding her efforts, and she enlisted several people who would hold her accountable. She backslid a little, but in the end she made progress. After several months, a typical day in Barbara's life looked more like this—

Free at Last

Barbara was rarely up past 10:30 P.M., and so when her alarm went off at 6:30 A.M. she was rested and prepared for the day. She had learned to keep up with the laundry by de-lumping (just one load of laundry a day kept her in clean clothes). No more digging through the dryer for a blouse or pulling a wrinkled skirt out of the dirty clothes. Her clothes were clean and neatly laid out each morning. She scheduled trips to the grocery store using her calendar, and thus was supplied with plenty of breakfast food. No more zipping under the golden arches on her mad dash to work.

Barbara made sure that projects were completed on time by sticking to her plan of working in thirty-minute segments. She learned how to set small goals that moved her toward the main goal. It made working on projects less intimidating, and her boss and co-workers noticed that she was focused and calm. She was on time to work in the mornings instead of stumbling in twenty minutes late with breakfast in one hand and her makeup bag in the other.

She found that the most satisfying thing about not procrastinating was the freedom from guilt. Barbara had spent much of her adult life feeling guilty for not getting things done. She felt like she was constantly letting other people down. She was intelligent and capable, but procrastination made her feel stupid and inadequate. When she was finally able to succeed in starting and finishing projects and doing things that she had spent most of her life trying to put off (laundry, writing letters, cleaning her house, getting the oil changed in her car), she suddenly saw herself in a new light. Her self-confidence soared and she had the courage to tackle projects and goals that she would have never thought possible.

Every now and then, she was tempted to fall into her old patterns, but after tasting the freedom of life without chronic procrastination, she couldn't imagine going back to her former ways.

Getting things done on a small scale gives us the confidence to tackle the bigger, weightier things in life that we've been putting off, like losing weight, quitting smoking, or dealing with a difficult relationship. When we have confidence that we can get small things done, then we are ready to address the larger issues in our life.

You may have big dreams that you have been putting off. The tools and methods outlined in this book give you a road map toward setting a goal and achieving it. There will still be many things in your life that are out of your control, but procrastination will not be one of them. As you successfully start, work on, and complete projects and goals, you will experience the freedom that comes with getting things done—now.

PERSONAL REFLECTION:

Think of a time when you successfully started and completed a project or task without the agony of procrastination. How did it feel? Think of a goal that you set for yourself, then never did get started on or finish. What are some of the emotions you felt?

✓ YOUR TO DO LIST:

Look back at the goal you wrote on the index card when you began this book. How are you progressing on it? Is it completed?

If you have not completed your goal, what has held you back? If you have completed it, reward yourself.

Continue on the path toward defeating your procrastination using the methods and tools outlined in this book.

FOR FURTHER STUDY:

The On-Time, On-Target Manager: How a "Last-Minute Manager" Conquered Procrastination
    —by Ken Blanchard and Steve Gottry

Isn't It About Time? How to Overcome Procrastination and Get on with Your Life
    —by Andrea Perry

NOTES

Chapter 1

[1] "Procrastination: Ten Things to Know."
www.psychologytoday.com/rss/pto-20030823-000001.html

[2] Dr. Kevin Austin, Web article:
www.counseling.caltech.edu/articles/procrastination.html

Chapter 2

[1] Robert B. Simmonds, PhD: "Just Do It! Confronting
Procrastination and Getting Things Done."
www.emotionalwellness.com/procrastination.htm

Chapter 3

[1] D.M. Tice and R.F. Baumeister, *Psychological Science*,
(1997, Volume 18): 454-458).

Chapter 4

[1] Diane and Julia Loomans, "Goal Setting: Making Dreams
Come True", Web article:
http://www.innerself.com/Parenting/goal_setting.htm.

Chapter 5

[1] "Perfectionism: A Doubled-Edged Sword," the Counseling and
Mental Health Center at the University of Texas at Austin:
www.utexas.edu/student/cmhc/booklets/perfection/perfect.

[2] Jane B. Burka and Lenora M. Yuen, PhD, *Procrastination: Why You
Do It, What to Do About It* (DaCapo Press, 1983), 20-21.

Chapter 6

[1] Camille B. Wortman, Elizabeth F. Loftus, Charles A. Weaver, III,
Psychology 5e. Excerpted from
www.mhhe.com/socscience/intro/cafe/wort/sg/chap12/sum.htm

Chapter 8

[1] Web article: www.goal-setting-guide.com/goal-writing

Chapter 9

[1] Burka and Yuen, *Procrastination*, 133-134.

[2] Dr. Timothy Quek. Web article:
www.address.org/article/procrastination/quek.php

[3] Barbara Sarason, "Procrastination May Be Dangerous to Your Health," (Peregrine Publishers, 1998).

[4] Scott Ginsberg, "Why I Can't Remember Your Name." Web article: www.hodu.com/name

Chapter 10

[1] Neil Fiore, *The Now Habit* (New York: Penguin Putnam, 1989).

Chapter 11

[1] Ginger Blume, "Psychology and Clutter." Web article:
www.drgingerblume.com/scripts_cluttered_life

[2] Web article excerpted on 10/19/2005 from *Organizing From the Inside Out* by Julie Morgenstern (Owl Books, 1998).

Chapter 12

[1] Fiore, *Now*, 82.

Chapter 13

[1] Dr. Robert B. Simmonds. Web article:
www.emotionalwellness.com

Chapter 14

[1] Web article:
www.server.carleton.ca/~tpychyl/prg/research history term.html

Chapter 15

[1] Dr. Gail Stalz, "Procrastinators: Don't put off reading this!" Web article: www.msnbc.msn.com/id/7399254

Chapter 16

[1] Dr. Piers Steel, "Putting Tasks Off Comes All Too Naturally," *Business Edge News Magazine* (June 19, 2003).

[2] Web article: www.psychologytoday.com/articles/pto-20030826-000017.html

Chapter 17

[1] David Jacobson, "The Danger in Delay," November 27, 2000. Web article: www.medicinenet.com/script/main/art.asp?articlekey=50853

BIBLIOGRAPHY

[1] Rita Emmett, *The Procrastinator's Handbook* (Walker & Company, 2000).